The Gi

Other books by Eugene H. Peterson
available from HarperCollins

The Journey – A Guidebook to the Pilgrim Life
Praying with Jesus
Praying with the Psalms
Praying with Moses
Praying with the Early Christians

THE GIFT
Reflections on a Christian Ministry

Marshall Pickering
An Imprint of HarperCollinsPublishers

Marshall Pickering is an Imprint of
HarperCollins*Religious*
Part of HarperCollins*Publishers*
77–85 Fulham Palace Road, London W6 8JB

Originally published in the USA in 1993 by
Wm B. Eerdmans Publishing Co.

First published in Great Britain
in 1995 by Marshall Pickering

1   3   5   7   9   10   8   6   4   2

A catalogue record for this book is
available from the British Library

ISBN 0 551 02978-1

Printed and bound in Great Britain by
HarperCollinsManufacturing Glasgow

Unless otherwise noted, Scripture quotations are from the
Revised Standard Version of the Bible, copyrighted 1946,
1952 © 1971, 1973 by the Division of Christian Education
of the National Council of the Churches of Christ in
the U.S.A., and used by permission.

For H. James Riddell
γνήσιος σύζυγος

Contents

REDEFINITIONS

BETWEEN SUNDAYS

THE WORD MADE FRESH

REDEFINITIONS

I

The Naked Noun

If I, even for a moment, accept my culture's definition of me, I am rendered harmless.

A HEALTHY noun doesn't need adjectives. Adjectives clutter a noun that is robust. But if the noun is culture-damaged or culture-diseased, adjectives are necessary.

"Pastor" used to be that kind of noun — energetic and virile. I have always loved the sound of the word. From an early age, the word called to mind a person who was passionate for God and compassionate with people. And even though the pastors I knew did not embody those characteristics, the word itself held its own against its exemplars. Today still, when people ask me what I want to be called, I always say, "Pastor."

But when I observe the way the vocation of pastor is lived out in America and listen to the tone and context in which the word *pastor* is spoken, I realize that what I hear in the word and what others hear is very different. In general usage, the noun is weak, defined by parody and diluted by opportunism. The need for strengthening adjectives is critical.

I find I have to exercise this adjectival rehabilitation constantly, redefining by refusing the definitions of *pastor* that the culture hands me, and reformulating my life with the insights and images of Scripture. The culture treats me so amiably! It encourages me to maintain my orthodox creed; it commends me for my evangelical practice; it praises me for my singular devotion. All it asks is that I accept its definition of my work as an encourager of the culture's good will, as the priest who will sprinkle holy water on the culture's good intentions. Many of these people are my friends. None, that I am aware of, is consciously malign.

But if I, even for a moment, accept my culture's definition of me, I am rendered harmless. I can denounce evil and stupidity all I wish and will be tolerated in my denunciations as a court jester is tolerated. I can organize their splendid goodwill and they will let me do it, since it is only for weekends.

The essence of being a pastor begs for redefinition. To that end, I offer three adjectives to clarify the noun: *unbusy, subversive, apocalyptic.*

II

The Unbusy Pastor

How can I persuade a person to live by faith and not by works if I have to juggle my schedule constantly to make everything fit into place?

THE ONE piece of mail certain to go unread into my waste-basket is the letter addressed to the "busy pastor." Not that the phrase doesn't describe me at times, but I refuse to give my attention to someone who encourages what is worst in me.

I'm not arguing the accuracy of the adjective; I am, though, contesting the way it's used to flatter and express sympathy.

"The poor man," we say. "He's so devoted to his flock; the work is endless, and he sacrifices himself so unstintingly." But the word *busy* is the symptom not of commitment but of betrayal. It is not devotion but defection. The adjective *busy* set as a modifier to *pastor* should sound to our ears like *adulterous* to characterize a wife or *embezzling* to describe a banker. It is an outrageous scandal, a blasphemous affront.

Hilary of Tours diagnosed our pastoral busyness as *ir-*

17

religiosa sollicitudo pro Deo, a blasphemous anxiety to do God's work for him.

I (and most pastors, I believe) become busy for two reasons; both are ignoble.

I am busy because I am vain. I want to appear important. Significant. What better way than to be busy? The incredible hours, the crowded schedule, and the heavy demands on my time are proof to myself — and to all who will notice — that I am important. If I go into a doctor's office and find there's no one waiting, and I see through a half-open door the doctor reading a book, I wonder if he's any good. A good doctor will have people lined up waiting to see him; a good doctor will not have time to read a book. Although I grumble about waiting my turn in a busy doctor's office, I am also impressed with his importance.

Such experiences affect me. I live in a society in which crowded schedules and harassed conditions are evidence of importance, so I develop a crowded schedule and harassed conditions. When others notice, they acknowledge my significance, and my vanity is fed.

I am busy because I am lazy. I indolently let others decide what I will do instead of resolutely deciding myself. I let people who do not understand the work of the pastor write the agenda for my day's work because I am too slipshod to write it myself. The pastor is a shadow figure in these people's minds, a marginal person vaguely connected with matters of God and good will. Anything remotely religious or somehow well-intentioned can be properly assigned to the pastor.

Because these assignments to pastoral service are made sincerely, I go along with them. It takes effort to refuse, and besides, there's always the danger that the refusal will be interpreted as a rebuff, a betrayal of religion, and a calloused disregard for people in need.

It was a favorite theme of C. S. Lewis that only lazy people work hard. By lazily abdicating the essential work of deciding and directing, establishing values and setting goals, other people do it for us; then we find ourselves frantically, at the last minute, trying to satisfy a half dozen different demands on our time, none of which is essential to our vocation, to stave off the disaster of disappointing someone.

But if I vainly crowd my day with conspicuous activity or let others fill my day with imperious demands, I don't have time to do my proper work, the work to which I have been called. How can I lead people into the quiet place beside the still waters if I am in perpetual motion? How can I persuade a person to live by faith and not by works if I have to juggle my schedule constantly to make everything fit into place?

Much Ado about the Significant

If I'm not busy making my mark in the world or doing what everyone expects me to do, what do I do? What is my proper work? What does it mean to be a pastor? If no one asked me to do anything, what would I do?

Three things.

I can be a pastor who prays. I want to cultivate my relationship with God. I want all of life to be intimate — sometimes consciously, sometimes unconsciously — with the God who made, directs, and loves me. And I want to waken others to the nature and centrality of prayer. I want to be a person in this community to whom others can come without hesitation, without wondering if it is appropriate, to get direction in prayer and praying. I want to do the original work of being in deepening conversation with the God who reveals himself to me and addresses me by name. I don't want to dispense mimeographed hand-outs that describe God's business; I want to witness out of my own experience. I don't want to live as a parasite on the first-hand spiritual life of others, but to be personally involved with all my senses, tasting and seeing that the Lord is good.

I know it takes time to develop a life of prayer: set-aside, disciplined, deliberate time. It isn't accomplished on the run, nor by offering prayers from a pulpit or at a hospital bedside. I know I can't be busy and pray at the same time. I can be active and pray; I can work and pray; but I cannot be busy and pray. I cannot be inwardly rushed, distracted, or dispersed. In order to pray I have to be paying more attention to God than to what people are saying to me; to God than to my clamoring ego. Usually, for that to happen there must be a deliberate withdrawal from the noise of the day, a disciplined detachment from the insatiable self.

I can be a pastor who preaches. I want to speak the Word of God that is Scripture in the language and rhythms of the people I live with. I am given an honored and protected time each week to do that. The pulpit is a great gift, and I want to use it well.

I have no interest in "delivering sermons," challenging people to face the needs of the day or giving bright, inspirational messages. With the help provided by scholars and editors, I can prepare a fairly respectable sermon of either sort in a few hours each week, a sermon that will pass muster with most congregations. They might not think it the greatest sermon, but they would accept it.

But what I want to do can't be done that way. I need a drenching in Scripture; I require an immersion in biblical studies. I need reflective hours over the pages of Scripture as well as personal struggles with the meaning of Scripture. That takes far more time than it takes to prepare a sermon.

I want the people who come to worship in my congregation each Sunday to hear the Word of God preached in such a way that they hear its distinctive note of authority as God's Word, and to know that their own lives are being addressed on their home territory. A sound outline and snappy illustrations don't make that happen.

This kind of preaching is a creative act that requires quietness and solitude, concentration and intensity. "All speech that moves men," contends R. E. C. Browne, "was minted when some man's mind was poised and still." I can't do that when I'm busy.

I can be a pastor who listens. A lot of people approach me through the week to tell me what's going on in their lives. I want to have the energy and time to really listen to them so that when they're through, they know at least one other person has some inkling of what they're feeling and thinking.

Listening is in short supply in the world today; people aren't used to being listened to. I know how easy it is to avoid the tough, intense work of listening by being busy — as when I let a hospital patient know there are ten more people I have to see. (Have to? I'm not indispensable to any of them, and I am here with this one.) Too much of pastoral visitation is punching the clock, assuring people we're on the job, being busy, earning our pay.

Pastoral listening requires unhurried leisure, even if it's only for five minutes. Leisure is a quality of spirit, not a quantity of time. Only in that ambiance of leisure do persons know they are listened to with absolute seriousness, treated with dignity and importance. Speaking to people does not have the same personal intensity as listening to them. The question I put to myself is not "How many people have you spoken to about Christ this week?" but "How many people have you listened to in Christ this week?" The number of persons listened to must necessarily be less than the number spoken to. Listening to a story always takes more time than delivering a message, so I must discard my compulsion to count, to compile the statistics that will justify my existence.

I can't listen if I'm busy. When my schedule is crowded, I'm not free to listen: I have to keep my next appointment; I have to get to the next meeting. But if I provide margins to my day, there is ample time to listen.

The Means to the Margins

"Yes, but how?" The appointment calendar is the tool with which to get unbusy. It's a gift of the Holy Ghost (unlisted by St. Paul, but a gift nonetheless) that provides the pastor with the means to get time and acquire leisure for praying, preaching, and listening. It is more effective than a protective secretary; it is less expensive than a retreat house. It is the one thing everyone in our society accepts without cavil as authoritative. The authority once given to Scripture is now ascribed to the appointment calendar. The dogma of verbal inerrancy has not been discarded, only re-assigned.

When I appeal to my appointment calendar, I am beyond criticism. If someone approaches me and asks me to pronounce the invocation at an event and I say, "I don't think I should do that; I was planning to use that time to pray," the response will be, "Well, I'm sure you can find another time to do that." But if I say, "My appointment calendar will not permit it," no further questions are asked. If someone asks me to attend a committee meeting and I say, "I was thinking of taking my wife out to dinner that night; I haven't listened to her carefully for several days," the response will be, "But you are very much needed at this meeting; couldn't you arrange another evening with your wife?" But if I say, "The appointment calendar will not permit it," there is no further discussion.

The trick, of course, is to get to the calendar before anyone else does. I mark out the times for prayer, for reading, for leisure, for the silence and solitude out of which creative work — prayer, preaching, and listening — can issue.

I find that when these central needs are met, there is plenty of time for everything else. And there is much else, for the pastor is not, and should not be, exempt from the hundred menial tasks or the administrative humdrum. These also are pastoral ministry. But the only way I have found to accomplish them without resentment and anxiety is to first take care of the priorities. If there is no time to nurture these essentials, I become a busy pastor, harassed and anxious, a whining, compulsive Martha instead of a contemplative Mary.

A number of years ago I was a busy pastor and had some back trouble that required therapy. I went for one hour sessions three times a week, and no one minded that I wasn't available for those three hours. Because the three hours had the authority of an appointment calendar behind them, they were sacrosanct.

On the analogy of that experience, I venture to prescribe appointments for myself to take care of the needs not only of my body, but also of my mind and emotions, my spirit and imagination. One week, in addition to daily half-hour conferences with St. Paul, my calendar reserved a two-hour block of time with Fyodor Dostoevsky. My spirit needed that as much as my body ten years ago needed the physical therapist. If nobody is going to prescribe it for me, I will prescribe it for myself.

The Poised Harpooner

In Herman Melville's *Moby Dick,* there is a turbulent scene in which a whaleboat scuds across a frothing ocean in pursuit of the great, white whale, Moby Dick. The sailors are laboring fiercely, every muscle taut, all attention and energy concentrated on the task. The cosmic conflict between good and evil is joined; chaotic sea and demonic sea monster versus the morally outraged man, Captain Ahab. In this boat, however, there is one man who does nothing. He doesn't hold an oar; he doesn't perspire; he doesn't shout. He is languid in the crash and the cursing. This man is the harpooner, quiet and poised, waiting. And then this sentence: "To insure the greatest efficiency in the dart, the harpooners of this world must start to their feet out of idleness, and not out of toil."

Melville's sentence is a text to set alongside the psalmist's "Be still, and know that I am God" (Ps. 46:10), and alongside Isaiah's "In returning and rest you shall be saved; in quietness and in trust shall be your strength" (Isa. 30:15).

Pastors know there is something radically wrong with the world. We are also engaged in doing something about it. The stimulus of conscience, the memory of ancient outrage, and the challenge of biblical command involve us in the anarchic sea that is the world. The white whale, symbol of evil, and the crippled captain, personification of violated righteousness, are joined in battle. History is a novel of spiritual conflict. In such a world, noise is inevitable, and immense energy is expended. But if there is no harpooner in the boat, there will be no proper finish to the chase. Or if the harpooner is exhausted, having abandoned his assignment and become an oarsman, he will not be ready and accurate when it is time to throw his javelin.

Somehow it always seems more compelling to assume the work of the oarsman, laboring mightily in a moral cause, throwing our energy into a fray we know has immortal consequence. And it always seems more dramatic to take on the outrage of a Captain Ahab, obsessed with a vision of vengeance and retaliation, brooding over the ancient injury done by the Enemy. There is, though, other important work to do. Someone must throw the dart. Some must be harpooners.

The metaphors Jesus used for the life of ministry are frequently images of the single, the small, and the quiet, which have effects far in excess of their appearance: salt, leaven, seed. Our culture publicizes the opposite emphasis: the big, the multitudinous, the noisy. It is, then, a strategic necessity that pastors deliberately ally themselves with the quiet, poised harpooners, and not leap, frenzied, to the oars. There is far more need that we develop the skills of the harpooner than the muscles of the oarsman. It is far more biblical to learn quietness and attentiveness before God than to be overtaken by what John Oman named the twin perils of ministry, "flurry and worry." For flurry dissipates energy, and worry constipates it.

Years ago I noticed, as all pastors must, that when a pastor left a neighboring congregation, the congregational life carried on very well, thank you. A guest preacher was assigned to conduct Sunday worship, and nearby pastors took care of the funerals, weddings, and crisis counseling. A congregation would go for months, sometimes as long as a year or two, without a regular pastor. And I thought, *All these things I am so busy doing — they aren't being done in that pastorless congregation, and nobody seems to mind.* I asked myself, *What if I, without leaving, quit doing them right now? Would anybody mind?* I did, and they don't.

III

The Subversive Pastor

I am undermining the kingdom of self and establishing the kingdom of God. I am being subversive.

As a pastor, I don't like being viewed as nice but insignificant. I bristle when a high-energy executive leaves the place of worship with the comment, "This was wonderful, Pastor, but now we have to get back to the real world, don't we?" I had thought we were in the most-real world, the world revealed as God's, a world believed to be invaded by God's grace and turning on the pivot of Christ's crucifixion and resurrection. The executive's comment brings me up short: he isn't taking this seriously. Worshiping God is marginal to making money. Prayer is marginal to the bottom line. Christian salvation is a brand preference.

I bristle and want to assert my importance. I want to force the recognition of the key position I hold in the economy of God and in *his* economy if only he knew it.

Then I remember that I am a subversive. My long-term effectiveness depends on my not being recognized for who I really am. If he realized that I actually believe the American way of life is doomed to destruction, and that another kingdom is right now being formed in secret to take its place, he wouldn't be at all pleased. If he knew what I was really doing and the difference it was making, he would fire me.

Yes, I believe that. I believe that the kingdoms of this world, American and Venezuelan and Chinese, will become the kingdom of our God and Christ, and I believe this new kingdom is already among us. That is why I'm a pastor, to introduce people to the real world and train them to live in it. I learned early that the methods of my work must correspond to the realities of the kingdom. The methods that make the kingdom of America strong — economic, military, technological, informational — are not suited to making the kingdom of God strong. I have had to learn a new methodology: truth-telling and love-making, prayer and parable. These are not methods very well adapted to raising the standard of living in suburbia or massaging the ego into a fashionable shape.

But America and suburbia and the ego compose my parish. Most of the individuals in this amalgam suppose that the goals they have for themselves and the goals God has for them are the same. It is the oldest religious mistake: refusing to countenance any real difference between God and us, imagining God to be a vague extrapolation of our own desires, and then hiring a priest to manage the affairs between self and the extrapolation. And I, one of the priests they hired, am having none of it.

But if I'm not willing to help them become what they want to be, what am I doing taking their pay? I am being subversive. I am undermining the kingdom of self and establishing the kingdom of God. I am helping them to become what God wants them to be, using the methods of subversion.

But isn't that dishonest? Not exactly, for I'm not misrepresenting myself. I'm simply taking my words and acts at a level of seriousness that would throw them into a state of catatonic disbelief if they ever knew.

The Pastor's Odd Niche

Pastors occupy an odd niche in American culture. Christian communities employ us to lead worship, teach and preach the Scriptures, and provide guidance and encouragement in the pilgrim way. Within our congregation, we experience a modest honor in our position. Occasionally one of us rises to national prominence and catches the attention of large numbers of people with the charisma of sunny, millennial cheerleading or (less often) the scary forecasts of Armageddon. But most of us are known by name only to our congregations and, except for ceremonial appearances at weddings, funerals, and bullroasts, are not in the public eye.

In general, people treat us with respect, but we are not considered important in any social, cultural, or economic way. In parody we are usually treated as harmless innocents, in satire as shiftless parasites.

This is not what most of us had in mind when we signed on. We had not counted on anything either so benign or so marginal. The images forming our pastoral expectations had a good deal more fierceness to them: Moses' bearding the Pharaoh; Jeremiah with fire in his mouth; Peter swashbucklingly reckless as the lead apostle; Paul's careering through prison and ecstasy, shipwreck and kerygma. The kingdom of God in which we had apprenticed ourselves was presented to us as revolutionary, a dangerously unwelcome intruder in the Old Boy Club of thrones, dominions, principalities, and powers.

The vocabulary we learned in preparation for our work was a language of battle ("We fight not against flesh and blood"), danger ("Your adversary the devil prowls around like a roaring lion, seeking some one to devour"), and austerity ("Take up your cross and follow me"). After arriving on the job, we find precious few opportunities to use our leadership language. And so, like the two years of Spanish we took in high school, it is soon nonfunctional from nonuse.

Did we learn the wrong language? Did we acquire the wrong images? Did we apprentice ourselves to the wrong master?

Everybody treats us so nicely. No one seems to think we mean what we say. When we say "kingdom of God," no one gets apprehensive, as if we had just announced (which we thought we had) that a powerful army is poised on the border, ready to invade. When we say radical things like "Christ," "love," "believe," "peace," "and "sin" — words that in other times and cultures excited martyrdoms — the sounds enter the stream of conversation with no more splash than baseball scores and grocery prices.

It's hard to maintain a self-concept as a revolutionary when everyone treats us with the same affability they give the grocer.

Are these people right? Is their way of life in no danger from us? Is what we say about God and his ways among us not real in the same way that Chevrolets and basketball teams and fresh garden spinach are real? Many pastors, realizing the opinion polls overwhelmingly repudiate their self-concept, submit to the cultural verdict and slip into the role of chaplain to the culture. It is easy to do. But some pastors do not; they become subversives in the culture.

Virginia Stem Owens has written the most powerful evocation since *King Lear* of the subversive character of the person (and this certainly includes the pastor) who intends to convert the world by truth and not guns. Her book *And the Trees Clap*

Their Hands is a dazzling performance on the parallel bars of anti-gnostic polemic and "God's spy" intrigue. In the opening pages, Owens, accompanied by her pastor-husband, sets the scene.

"We sit in coffee shops and scan faces as they filter by unawares on the sidewalk. We are collecting, sorting, storing the data. But we do not call ourselves scientists; we cannot make controlled experiments. In life there can never be a control group. There is only what is — or what presents itself, at any given moment, for our perusal. And we, with our own limitations, can only be in one place and one time at any moment. For this reason we call ourselves spies, for we must strike a trail and stick to it. We must catch as catch can, life being no laboratory, spreading our senses wide and drawing them in again to study what we have managed to snare in the wind.

"We have several covers, my companion and I, business we appear to be about while we are actually always watching for signs of the invisible prey, which is our primary occupation. He, for example, balances church budgets, counsels divorcees and delinquents, writes sermons. But beneath it all is a constant watchfulness, a taking note. Even as he stands in the pulpit, he sifts the faces of the congregation for those fine grains, no larger than the dust of pollen, that carry the spoor of the trail he's on.

"And I sit among them there, internally knitting them up like Madame Defarge, listening, recording, watching, remembering. Softly. Softly. The clues one must go on are often small and fleeting. A millimeter's widening of the eye, a faint contraction of the nostrils, a silent exhalation, the slight upward modulation of the voice. To spy out the reality hidden in appearances requires vigilance, perseverance. It takes everything I've got."

The kingdom of self is heavily defended territory. Post-Eden Adams and Eves are willing to pay their respects to God, but they don't want him invading their turf. Most sin, far from being a mere lapse of morals or a weak will, is an energetically and expensively erected defense against God. Direct assault in an openly declared war on the god-self is extraordinarily ineffective. Hitting sin head-on is like hitting a nail with a hammer; it only drives it in deeper. There are occasional exceptions, strategically dictated confrontations, but indirection is the biblically preferred method.

Jesus the Subversive

Jesus was a master at subversion. Until the very end, everyone, including his disciples, called him Rabbi. Rabbis were important, but they didn't make anything happen. On the occasions when suspicions were aroused that there might be more to him than that title accounted for, Jesus tried to keep it quiet — "Tell no one."

Jesus' favorite speech form, the parable, was subversive. Parables sound absolutely ordinary: casual stories about soil and seeds, meals and coins and sheep, bandits and victims, farmers and merchants. And they are wholly secular: of his forty or so parables recorded in the Gospels, only one has its setting in church, and only a couple mention the name God. As people heard Jesus tell these stories, they saw at once that they weren't about God, so there was nothing in them threatening their own sovereignty. They relaxed their defenses. They walked away perplexed, wondering what they meant, the stories lodged in their imagination. And then, like a time bomb, they would explode in their unprotected hearts. An abyss opened up at their very feet. He *was* talking about God; they had been invaded!

Jesus continually threw odd stories down alongside ordinary lives (*para,* "alongside"; *bole,* "thrown") and walked away without explanation or altar call. Then listeners started seeing connections: God connections, life connections, eternity connections. The very lack of obviousness, the unlikeness, was the stimulus to perceiving likeness: God likeness, life likeness, eternity likeness. But the parable didn't do the work — it put the listener's imagination to work. Parables aren't illustrations that make things easier; they make things harder by requiring the exercise of our imaginations, which if we aren't careful becomes the exercise of our faith.

Parables subversively slip past our defenses. Once they're inside the citadel of self, we might expect a change of method, a sudden brandishing of bayonets resulting in a palace coup. But it doesn't happen. Our integrity is honored and preserved. God does not impose his reality from without; he grows flowers and fruit from within. God's truth is not an alien invasion but a loving courtship in which the details of our common lives are treated as seeds in our conception, growth, and maturity in the kingdom. Parables trust our imaginations, which is to say, our faith. They don't herd us paternalistically into a classroom where we get things explained and diagrammed. They don't bully us into regiments where we find ourselves marching in a moral goose step.

There is hardly a detail in the gospel story that was not at the time (and still) overlooked because unlikely, dismissed because commonplace, and rejected because illegal. But under the surface of conventionality and behind the scenes of probability, each was effectively inaugurating the kingdom: illegitimate (as was supposed) conception, barnyard birth, Nazareth silence, Galilean secularity, Sabbath healings, Gethsemane prayers, criminal death, baptismal water, eucharistic bread and wine. Subversion.

The Assumptions of Subversives

Three things are implicit in subversion. One, the status quo is wrong and must be overthrown if the world is going to be livable. It is so deeply wrong that repair work is futile. The world is, in the word insurance agents use to designate our wrecked cars, totaled.

Two, there is another world aborning that is livable. Its reality is no chimera. It is in existence, though not visible. Its character is known. The subversive does not operate out of a utopian dream but out of a conviction of the nature of the real world.

Three, the usual means by which one kingdom is thrown out and another put in its place — military force or democratic elections — are not available. If we have neither a preponderance of power nor a majority of votes, we begin searching for other ways to effect change. We discover the methods of subversion. We find and welcome allies.

At a sixtieth birthday conversation in 1986, the poet A. R. Ammons was asked, "Is poetry subversive?" He responded, "Yes, you have no idea how subversive — deeply subversive. Consciousness often reaches a deeply intense level at the edges of things, questioning and undermining accepted ways of doing things. The audience resists change to the last moment, and then is grateful for it."

These are the convictions implicit in the gospel. They are not, though, convictions commonly implicit in parish life. More frequently, there is the untested assumption that the congregation is close to being the kingdom already and that if we all pull together and try a little harder, it will be. Pastors especially seem to assume that everybody, or at least a majority, in a congregation can be either persuaded or pushed into righteousness and maybe even holiness, in spite of centuries of evidence to the contrary.

That pastors need an accurate knowledge of Christian

doctrine is universally acknowledged; that they need practiced skill in the techniques of Christian subversion is a minority conviction. But Jesus is the Way as well as the Truth. The way the gospel is conveyed is as much a part of the kingdom as the truth presented. Why are pastors experts on the truth and dropouts on the way?

In acquiring familiarity and skill in pastoral subversion, we could do worse than to read spy novels and observe the strategies of communist infiltration, but the biblical passages are more than adequate if we will only pay attention to them:

- "A great and strong wind rent the mountains, and broke in pieces the rocks before the Lord, but the Lord was not in the wind; and after the wind an earthquake, but the Lord was not in the earthquake; and after the earthquake a fire, but the Lord was not in the fire; and after the fire a still small voice" (1 Kings 19:11–12).

- "This is the word of the Lord to Zerubbabel: Not by might, nor by power, but by my Spirit, says the Lord of hosts" (Zech. 4:6).

- "You are the salt of the earth" (Matt. 5:13).

- "The kingdom of heaven is like a grain of mustard seed which a man took and sowed in his field; it is the smallest of all seeds" (Matt. 13:31–32).

- "For I decided to know nothing among you except Jesus Christ and him crucified. And I was with you in weakness and in much fear and trembling" (1 Cor. 2:2–3).

Unfortunately, this unbroken biblical methodology of subversion is easily and frequently discarded by pastors in favor of assault or promotion. There are two likely reasons: vanity and naiveté.

Vanity. We don't like being wallflowers at the world's party. A recent study of the decline in white males' preparing for pastoral work concluded that a major reason is that there's no prestige left in the job. Interestingly, the slack is taken up by others (blacks, Asians, women) who apparently are not looking for prestige and have a history of working subversively. Neither was there prestige in Paul's itinerant tent-making.

Naiveté. We think the church is already the kingdom of God and, if only better organized and motivated, can conquer the world. But nowhere in Scripture or history do we see a church synonymous with the kingdom of God. The church in many instances is more worldly than the world. When we equate the church and the kingdom and the identity turns out to be false, we feel "taken in." Little wonder that anger and cynicism are epidemic behind the smiling veneer of American pastors. We need refresher courses in Barthian critiques of religion and Dantean analyses of sin, especially spiritual sin.

Tools of Subversion

Prayer and parable are the stock-in-trade tools of the subversive pastor. The quiet (or noisy) closet life of prayer enters into partnership with the Spirit that strives still with every human heart, a wrestling match in holiness. And parables are the consciousness-altering words that slip past falsifying platitude and invade the human spirit with Christ-truth.

This is our primary work in the real world. But we need continual convincing. The people for whom we are praying and among whom we are telling parables are seduced into supposing that their money and ambition are making the world turn on its axis. There are so many of them and so few of us, making it difficult to maintain our convictions. It is easy to be seduced along with them.

Words are the real work of the world — prayer words with God, parable words with men and women. The behind-the-scenes work of creativity by word and sacrament, by parable and prayer, subverts the seduced world. The pastor's real work is what Ivan Illich calls "shadow work" — the work nobody gets paid for and few notice but that makes a world of salvation: meaning and value and purpose, a world of love and hope and faith — in short, the kingdom of God.

IV

The Apocalyptic Pastor

With the vastness of the heavenly invasion and the urgency of the faith decision rolling into our consciousness like thunder and lightning, we cannot stand around on Sunday morning filling the time with pretentious small talk on how bad the world is and how wonderful this new stewardship campaign is going to be.

THE ADJECTIVE *apocalyptic* is not commonly found in company with the noun *pastor.* I can't remember ever hearing them in the same sentence. They grew up on different sides of the tracks. I'd like to play Cupid between the two words and see if I can instigate a courtship.

Apocalyptic has a wild sound to it: an end-of-the-world craziness; a catastrophic urgency. The word is used when history seems out of control and ordinary life is hopeless. When you aren't sure whether it is bombs or stars that are failing out of the sky, and people are rushing toward the cliffs like a herd of pigs, the scene is "apocalyptic." The word is scary and unsettling.

Pastor is a comforting word: a person who confidently quotes the Twenty-third Psalm when you are shivering in the dark shadows. Pastors gather us in quiet adoration before God. Pastors represent the faithfulness and love of the eternal God and show up on time every Sunday to say it again — that God so loves the world. Pastors build bridges over troubled waters and guide wandering feet back to the main road. The word accumulates associations of security and blessing, solidity and peace.

But I have a biblical reason for bringing the two words together. The last book of the Bible was written by a pastor. And the book he wrote was an apocalypse. The St. John who gave us the last words of the Bible was an apocalyptic pastor.

I am misunderstood by most of the people who call me pastor. Their misunderstandings are contagious, and I find myself misunderstanding: Who am I? What is my proper work? I look around. I ask questions. I scout the American landscape for images of pastoral work. What does a pastor do? What does a pastor look like? What place does a pastor occupy in church and culture? I get handed a job description that seems to have been developed from the latest marketing studies of religious consumer needs. But there are no images, no stories. St. John gives me an image and a story — and a blessedly blank job description. He is my candidate for patron saint for pastors.

St. John is the kind of pastor I would like to be. My admiration expands: he is also the kind of pastor I would like my colleagues to be. As I look to him, searching for the energy source that makes him a master and not one more religious hack, I find it is the apocalyptic element that is critical.

Ernst Käsemann captured what many think is *the* unique biblical stance in his sentence: "Apocalyptic was the mother of all Christian theology." Perhaps, then, the grandmother of all Christian pastoral work. Early church Christians believed that the resurrection of Jesus inaugurated a new age. They were in fact — but against appearances — living in God's kingdom, a kingdom of truth and healing and grace. This was all actually present but hidden from unbelieving eyes and inaudible to unbelieving ears.

Pastors are the persons in the church communities who repeat and insist on these kingdom realities against the world appearances, and who therefore must be apocalyptic. In its dictionary meaning, apocalypse is simply "revelation," the uncovering of what was covered up so that we can see what is there. But the context in which the word arrives adds color to the black-and-white dictionary meaning, colors bright and dark — crimson urgency and purple crisis. Under the crisis of persecution and under the urgency of an imminent end, reality is revealed suddenly for what it is. We had supposed our lives were so utterly *ordinary*. Sin-habits dull our free faith into stodgy moralism and respectable boredom; then crisis rips the veneer of cliché off everyday routines and reveals the side-by-side splendors and terrors of heaven and hell. Apocalypse is arson — it secretly sets a fire in the imagination that boils the fat out of an obese culture-religion and renders a clear gospel love, a pure gospel hope, a purged gospel faith.

I have been a pastor for thirty years to American Christians who do their best to fireproof themselves against crisis and urgency. Is there any way that I can live with these people and love them without being shaped by the golden-calf culture? How can I keep from settling into the salary and benefits of a checkout clerk in a store for religious consumers? How can I avoid a metamorphosis from the holy vocation of pastor into a promising career in religious sales?

Here is a way: submit my imagination to St. John's apocalypse — the crisis of the End combined with the urgencies of God — and let the energies of the apocalyptic define and shape me as pastor. When I do that, my life as pastor simplifies into prayer, poetry, and patience.

Apocalyptic Prayer

The apocalyptic pastor *prays*. St. John's pastoral vocation was worked out on his knees. He embraced the act of prayer as pivotal in his work, and then showed it as pivotal in everyone's work. Nothing a pastor does is different in kind from what all Christians do, but sometimes it is more focused, more visible. Prayer is the pivot action in the Christian community.

After a few introductory sentences in the Revelation, we come upon St. John in the place and practice of prayer (1:9–10). The place: "on the island called Patmos." The practice: "in the Spirit on the Lord's Day." In the intricate task of being pastor to his seven congregations, which in the case study we have before us involves composing this theological poem, *The Revelation,* he never leaves the place of prayer, never abandons the practice of prayer. At the end of the book he is still praying: "Amen. Come, Lord Jesus!" (22:20). St. John listens to God, is silent before God, sings to God, asks questions of God. The listening and silence, the songs and questions are wonderfully in touch with reality, mixing the sights and sounds of Roman affairs with the sights and sounds of salvation — angels and markets and Caesars and Jesus. St. John doesn't miss much. He is an alert and alive pastor. He reads and assimilates the Scriptures; he reads and feels the impact of the daily news. But neither ancient Scripture nor current event is left the way it arrives on his doorstep; it is all turned into prayer.

St. John lives on the boundary of the invisible world of the Holy Spirit and the visible world of Roman times. On that boundary he prays. The praying is a joining of realities, making a live connection between the place we find ourselves and the God who is finding us.

But prayer is not a work that pastors are often asked to do except in ceremonial ways. Most pastoral work actually erodes prayer. The reason is obvious: people are not comfortable with God in their lives. They prefer something less awesome and more informal. Something, in fact, like the pastor. Reassuring, accessible, easygoing. People would rather talk to the pastor than to God. And so it happens that without anyone actually intending it, prayer is pushed to the sidelines.

And so pastors, instead of practicing prayer, which brings people into the presence of God, enter into the practice of messiah: we will do the work of God for God, fix people up, tell them what to do, conspire in finding the shortcuts by which the long journey to the Cross can be bypassed since we all have such crowded schedules right now. People love us when we do this. It is flattering to be put in the place of God. It feels wonderful to be treated in this godlike way. And it is work that we are generally quite good at.

A sense of apocalypse blows the whistle on such messianic pastoring. The vastness of the heavenly invasion, the urgency of the faith decision, the danger of the impinging culture — with these pouring into our consciousness accompanied by thunder and lightning, we cannot stand around on the street corners of Sunday morning filling the time with pretentious small talk on how bad the world is and how wonderful this new stewardship campaign is going to be.

If we have even an inkling of apocalypse, it will be impossible to act like the jaunty foreman of a home-improvement work crew that is going to re-landscape moral (or immoral) garden spots. We must pray. The world has been invaded by God, and it is with God we have to do.

Prayer is the most thoroughly *present* act we have as

humans, and the most energetic: it sockets the immediate past into the immediate future and makes a flexible, living joint of them. The Amen gathers what has just happened into the Maranatha of the about to happen and produces a Benediction. We pay attention to God and lead others to pay attention to God. It hardly matters that so many people would rather pay attention to their standards of living, or their self-image, or their zeal to make a mark in the world.

Apocalypse opens up the chasm of reality. The reality is God: worship or flee.

Apocalyptic Poet

The apocalyptic pastor is a *poet*. St. John was the first major poet of the Christian church. He used words in new ways, making (*poétés* in Greek is *maker*) truth right before our eyes, fresh in our ears. The way a pastor uses the language is a critical element in the work. The Christian gospel is rooted in language: God *spoke* a creation into being; our Savior was the *Word* made flesh. The poet is the person who uses words not primarily to convey information but to *make* a relationship, *shape* beauty, *form* truth. This is St. John's work; it is every pastor's work.

I do not mean that all pastors write poems or speak in rhyme, but that they treat words with reverence, stand in awe before not only the Word, but words, and realize that language itself partakes of the sacred.

If St. John's Revelation is not read as a poem, it is virtually incomprehensible, which, in fact, is why it is so often uncomprehended. St. John, playful with images and exuberant in metaphor, works his words into vast, rhythmic repetitions. The gospel has already been adequately proclaimed to these people to whom he is pastor; they have become Christians through preaching and teaching that originated with Peter and Paul, and was then passed on by canonical Gospel writers along with unnumbered deacons, elders, and martyrs. But there is more to St. John's work than making a cognitive connection with the sources. As pastor he re-speaks, re-visions the gospel so that his congregations experience the *word*, not mere words. To do that he must be a poet.

The pastor's task is to shape the praying imagination before the gospel. This revelation of God to us in Jesus is a fact so large and full of energy, and our capacities to believe and love and hope are so atrophied, that we need help to hear the words in their power, see the images in their energy.

Isn't it odd that pastors, who are responsible for interpreting the Scriptures, so much of which come in the form of poetry, have so little interest in poetry? It is a crippling defect and must be remedied. The Christian communities as a whole must rediscover poetry, and the pastors must lead them. Poetry is essential to the pastoral vocation because poetry is original speech. The word is creative: it brings into being what was not there before — perception, relationship, belief. Out of the silent abyss a sound is formed: people hear what was not heard before and are changed by the sound from loneliness into love. Out of the blank abyss a picture is formed by means of metaphor: people see what they did not see before and are changed by the image from anonymity into love. Words create. God's word creates; our words can participate in the creation.

But poetry is not the kind of language that pastors are asked to use, except in quotation at funerals. Most pastoral work erodes poetry. The reason is obvious: people are not comfortable with the uncertainties and risks and travail of creativity. It takes too much time. There is too much obscurity. People are more comfortable with prose. They prefer explanations of Bible history and information on God. This is appealing to the pastor, for we have a lot of information to hand out and are adept at explanations. After a few years of speaking in prose, we become prosaic.

Then a dose of apocalyptic stops us in mid-sentence: the power of the word to create faith, the force of imagination to resist the rationalism of evil, the necessity of shaping a people who speak and listen personally in worship and witness. The urgencies of apocalyptic shake us down to the roots of language, and we become poets: pay attention to core language, to personal language, to scriptural language.

Not all words create. Some merely communicate. They explain, report, describe, manage, inform, regulate. We live in an age obsessed with communication. Communication is good but a minor good. Knowing about things never has seemed to improve our lives a great deal. The pastoral task with words is not communication but communion — the healing and restoration and creation of love relationships between God and his fighting children and our fought-over creation. Poetry uses words in and for communion.

This is hard work and requires alertness. The language of our time is in terrible condition. It is used carelessly and cynically. Mostly it is a tool for propaganda, whether secular or religious. Every time badly used and abused language is carried by pastors into prayers and preaching and direction, the word of God is cheapened. We cannot use a bad means to a good end.

Words *making* truth, not just conveying it: liturgy and story and song and prayer are the work of pastors who are poets.

Apocalyptic Patience

The apocalyptic pastor is *patient*. St. John identified himself to his parishioners as "your brother, who shares with you in Jesus the tribulation and the kingdom and the patient endurance" (1:9). The "patient endurance," what the Greeks called *hypomone* — the hanging in there, the sticking it out — is one of the unexpected but most notable achievements of apocalyptic.

The connection is not obvious. After all, if everything is falling apart, and the world about to come to an end, doesn't that mean the end of patience? Why not cut and run? Why not eat, drink, and be merry for tomorrow we die? Bastard apocalyptic, apocalyptic that has no parentage in biblical sources or gospel commitments, does promote a progeny of irresponsibility (and the brats are noisily and distressingly in evidence on every American street), but the real thing, the conceived-in-holy-wedlock apocalyptic, develops communities that are passionately patient, courageously committed to witness and work in the kingdom of God no matter how long it takes, or how much it costs. Typically, marginal, oppressed, and exploited groups are nurtured on apocalypse.

St. John is terrifically urgent, but he is not in a hurry. Note his unhurried urgency in the book he wrote. It takes a long time to read *The Revelation*. It cannot be read quickly and requires repeated rereadings to enter into the subtle and glorious poem-vision. St. John works with vast and leisurely repetitions, pulling us into ancient rhythms. An impatient person never finishes this book. We learn patience in the very act of reading/listening to St. John's Apocalypse. If St. John would have been impatient, he would have given us a slogan on a decal.

The reason St. John insists on patience is that he is dealing with the vast mysteries of God and the intricacies of the messy human condition. This is going to take some time. Neither the mysteries nor the mess is simple. If we are going to learn a life of holiness in the mess of history, we are going to have to prepare for something intergenerational and think in centuries.

The apocalyptic imagination gives us a facility in what geologists call "deep time" — a sense of "ages" that transcends the compulsions of time-management experts and at the same time dignifies the existence of the meanest fossil.

But the working environment of pastors erodes patience and rewards impatience. People are uncomfortable with mystery (God) and mess (themselves). They avoid both mystery and mess by devising programs and hiring pastors to manage them. A program provides a defined structure with an achievable goal. Mystery and mess are eliminated at a stroke. This is appealing. In the midst of the mysteries of grace and the complexities of human sin, it is nice to have something that you can evaluate every month or so and find out where you stand. We don't have to deal with ourselves or with God, but can use the vocabulary of religion and work in an environment that acknowledges God, and so be assured that we are doing something significant.

With programs shaping the agenda — not amazing grace, not stubborn sin — the pastor doesn't have to be patient. We set a goal, work out a strategy, recruit a few Christian soldiers, and go to it. If, in two or three years the soldiers haven't produced, we shake the dust off our feet and hire on as captain to another group of mercenaries. When a congregation no longer serves our ambition, it is abandoned for another under the euphemism of "a larger ministry." In the majority of such cases, our impatience is rewarded with a larger salary.

Apocalypse shows this up as inexcusable exploitation. Apocalypse convinces us that we are in a desperate situation, and in it together. The grass is not greener in the next committee, or parish, or state. All that matters is worshiping God, dealing with evil, and developing faithfulness. Apocalypse ignites a sense of urgency, but it quenches shortcuts and hurry, for the times are in God's hands. Providence, not the newspaper, accounts for the times in which we live.

Impatience, the refusal to *endure,* is to pastoral character what strip mining is to the land — a greedy rape of what can be gotten at the least cost, and then abandonment in search of another place to loot. Something like fidelity comes out of apocalyptic: fidelity to God, to be sure, but also to people, to parish — to *place.*

St. John was patient, teaching the Christians in his seven less-than-promising congregations to be patient. But it is an apocalyptic patience — not acquiescence to boredom, not doormat submissiveness. It is giant sequoia patience that scorns the reduction of a glorious gospel to a fast-food religion. Mount Rainier patience that mocks the fast-lane frenzy for a weekend with the Spirit. How long did it take to grow the sequoia? How long did it take to build Rainier? Apocalypse ushers us into the long and the large. We acquire, with St. John and his congregations, fidelity to place and people, the faithful endurance that is respectful of the complexities of living a moral, spiritual, and liturgical life before the mysteries of God in the mess of history.

American religion is conspicuous for its messianically pretentious energy, its embarrassingly banal prose, and its impatiently hustling ambition. None of these marks is remotely biblical. None is faintly in evidence in the gospel story. All of them are thoroughly documented diseases of the spirit. Pastors are in great danger of being undetected carriers of the very disease we are charged to diagnose and heal. We need the most powerful of prophylactics — something like the apocalyptic prayer and poetry and patience of St. John.

BETWEEN SUNDAYS

V

Ministry amid the Traffic

From Monday through Saturday, the vision of myself as pastor, so clear in Lord's Day worship, is now blurred and distorted as it is reflected back from the eyes of confused and hurting people.

SUNDAYS are easy. The sanctuary is clean and orderly, the symbolism clear, the people polite. I know what I am doing: I am going to lead this people in worship, proclaim God's word to them, celebrate the sacraments. I have had time to prepare my words and spirit. And the people are ready, arriving dressed up and expectant. Centuries of tradition converge in this Sunday singing of hymns, exposition of Scripture, commitments of faith, offering of prayers, baptizing, eating and drinking the life of our Lord. I love doing this. I wake up early Sunday mornings, the adrenaline pumping into my veins.

But after the sun goes down on Sunday, the clarity diffuses. From Monday through Saturday, an unaccountably unruly people track mud through the holy places, leaving a mess. The order of worship gives way to the disorder of argument and

53

doubt, bodies in pain and emotions in confusion, misbehaving children and misdirected parents. I don't know what I am doing half the time. I am interrupted. I am asked questions to which I have no answers. I am put in situations for which I am not adequate. I find myself attempting tasks for which I have neither aptitude nor inclination. The vision of myself as pastor, so clear in Lord's Day worship, is now blurred and distorted as it is reflected back from the eyes of people who view me as pawn to their egos. The affirmations I experience in Sunday greetings are now precarious in the slippery mud of put-down and fault-finding.

Sundays are important — celebrative and essential. The first day defines and energizes our lives by means of our Lord's resurrection and gives a resurrection shape to the week. But the six days between Sundays are just as important, if not so celebrative, for they are the days to which the resurrection shape is given. Since most pastoral work takes place on the six days, an equivalent attention must be given to them, practicing the art of prayer in the middle of the traffic.

VI

Curing Souls: The Forgotten Art

Blessed are the poor in spirit

A beech tree in winter, white
Intricacies unconcealed
Against sky blue and billowed
Clouds, carries in his emptiness
Ripeness: sap ready to rise
On signal, buds alert to burst
To leaf. And then after a season
Of summer a lean ring to remember
The lush fulfilled promises.
Empty again in wise poverty
That lets the reaching branches stretch
A millimeter more towards heaven,
The bole expand ever so slightly
And push roots into the firm
Foundation, lucky to be leafless:
Deciduous reminder to let it go.

Areformation may be in process in the way pastors do their work. It may turn out to be as significant as the theological reformation of the sixteenth century. I hope so. The signs are accumulating.

The Reformers recovered the biblical doctrine of justification by faith. The gospel proclamation, fresh and personal and direct, through the centuries had become an immense, lumbering Rube Goldberg mechanism: elaborately contrived ecclesiastical gears, pulleys, and levers rumbled and creaked importantly but ended up doing something completely trivial. The Reformers recovered the personal passion and clarity so evident in Scripture. This rediscovery of firsthand involvement resulted in freshness and vigor.

The vocational reformation of our own time (if it turns out to be that) is a rediscovery of the pastoral work of the cure of souls. The phrase sounds antique. It is antique. But it is not obsolete. It catches up and coordinates, better than any other expression I am aware of, the unending warfare against sin and sorrow and the diligent cultivation of grace and faith to which the best pastors have consecrated themselves in every generation. The odd sound of the phrase may even work to advantage by calling attention to how remote present-day pastoral routines have become.

I am not the only pastor who has discovered this old identity. More and more pastors are embracing this way of pastoral work and are finding themselves authenticated by it. There are not a lot of us. We are by no means a majority, not even a high-profile minority. But one by one, pastors are rejecting the job description that has been handed to them and are taking on this new one or, as it turns out, the old one that has been in use for most of the Christian centuries.

It is not sheer fantasy to think there may come a time when the number reaches critical mass and effects a genuine vocational reformation among pastors. Even if it doesn't, it seems to me the single most significant and creative thing happening in pastoral ministry today.

There's a distinction between what pastors do on Sundays and what we do between Sundays. What we do on Sundays has not really changed through the centuries: proclaiming the gospel, teaching Scripture, celebrating the sacraments, offering prayers. But the work between Sundays has changed radically, and it has not been a development but a defection.

Until about a century ago, what pastors did between Sundays was a piece with what they did on Sundays. The context changed: instead of an assembled congregation, the pastor was with one other person or with small gatherings of persons, or alone in study and prayer. The manner changed: instead of proclamation, there was conversation. But the work was the same: discovering the meaning of Scripture, developing a life of prayer, guiding growth into maturity.

This is the pastoral work that is historically termed the cure of souls. The primary sense of *cura* in Latin is "care," with undertones of "cure." The soul is the essence of the human personality. The cure of souls, then, is the Scripture-directed, prayer-shaped care that is devoted to persons singly or in groups, in settings sacred and profane. It is a determination to work at the center, to concentrate on the essential.

The between-Sundays work of American pastors in this century, though, is running a church. I first heard the phrase just a few days before my ordination. After thirty years, I can still remember the unpleasant impression it made.

I was traveling with a pastor I respected very much. I was full of zest and vision, anticipating pastoral life. My inner conviction of call to the pastorate was about to be confirmed by others. What God wanted me to do, what I wanted to do, and what others wanted me to do were about to converge.

From fairly extensive reading about pastor and priest predecessors, I was impressed that everyday pastoral life was primarily concerned with developing a life of prayer among the people. Leading worship, preaching the gospel, and teaching Scripture on Sundays would develop in the next six days into representing the life of Christ in the human traffic of the everyday.

With my mind full of these thoughts, my pastor friend and I stopped at a service station for gasoline. My friend, a gregarious person, bantered with the attendant. Something in the exchange provoked a question.

"What do you do?"

"I run a church."

No answer could have surprised me more. I knew, of course, that pastoral life included institutional responsibilities, but it never occurred to me that I would be defined by those responsibilities. But the moment I became ordained, I found I was so defined both by the pastors and executives over me and by the parishioners around me. The first job description given me omitted prayer entirely.

Behind my back, while my pastoral identity was being formed by Gregory and Bernard, Luther and Calvin, Richard Baxter of Kidderminster and Nicholas Ferrar of Little Gidding, George Herbert and Jonathan Edwards, John Henry Newman and Alexander Whyte, Phillips Brooks and George MacDonald, the work of the pastor had been almost completely secularized (except for Sundays). I didn't like it and decided, after an interval of confused disorientation, that being a physician of souls took priority over running a church, and that I would be guided in my pastoral vocation by wise predecessors rather than contemporaries. Luckily, I have found allies along the way and a readiness among my parishioners to work with me in changing my pastoral job description.

It should be clear that the cure of souls is not a specialized form of ministry (analogous, for instance, to hospital chaplain or pastoral counselor) but is the essential pastoral work. It is not a narrowing of pastoral work to its devotional aspects, but it is a way of life that uses weekday tasks, encounters, and situations as the raw material for teaching prayer, developing faith, and preparing for a good death. Curing souls is a term that filters out what is introduced by a secularizing culture. It is also a term that identifies us with our ancestors and colleagues in ministry, lay and clerical, who are convinced that a life of prayer is the connective tissue between holy day proclamation and weekday discipleship.

A caveat: I contrast the cure of souls with the task of running a church, but I do not want to be misunderstood. I am not contemptuous of running a church, nor do I dismiss its importance. I run a church myself; I have for over twenty years. I try to do it well.

But I do it in the same spirit that I, along with my wife, run our house. There are many essential things we routinely do, often (but not always) with joy. But running a house is not what we do. What we do is build a home, develop in marriage, raise children, practice hospitality, pursue lives of work and play. It is reducing pastoral work to institutional duties that I object to, not the duties themselves, which I gladly share with others in the church.

It will hardly do, of course, to stubbornly defy the expectations of people and eccentrically go about pastoral work like a seventeenth-century curate, even if the eccentric curate is far more sane than the current clergy. The recovery of this essential between-Sundays work of the pastor must be worked out in tension with the secularized expectations of this age: there must be negotiation, discussion, experimentation, confrontation, adaptation. Pastors who devote themselves to the guidance of souls must do it among people who expect them to run a church. In a determined and kindly tension with those who thoughtlessly presume to write job descriptions for us, we can, I am convinced, recover our proper work.

Pastors, though, who decide to reclaim the vast territory of the soul as their preeminent responsibility will not do it by going away for job retraining. We must work it out on the job, for it is not only ourselves but our people whom we are desecularizing. The task of vocational recovery is as endless as theological reformation. Details vary with pastor and parish, but there are three areas of contrast between running a church and the cure of souls that all of us experience: initiative, language, and problems.

Initiative

In running the church, I seize the initiative. I take charge. I take responsibility for motivation and recruitment, for showing the way, for getting things started. If I don't, things drift. I am aware of the tendency to apathy, the human susceptibility to indolence, and I use my leadership position to counter it.

By contrast, the cure of souls is a cultivated awareness that God has already seized the initiative. The traditional doctrine defining this truth is prevenience: God everywhere and always seizing the initiative. He gets things going. He had and continues to have the first word. Prevenience is the conviction that God has been working diligently, redemptively, and strategically before I appeared on the scene, before I was aware there was something here for me to do.

The cure of souls is not indifferent to the realities of human lethargy, naive about congregational recalcitrance, or inattentive to neurotic cussedness. But there is a disciplined, determined conviction that everything (and I mean, precisely, everything) we do is a response to God's first work, his initiating act. We learn to be attentive to the divine action already in process so that the previously unheard word of God is heard, the previously unattended act of God is noticed.

Running-the-church questions are: What do we do? How can we get things going again?

Cure-of-souls questions are: What has God been doing here? What traces of grace can I discern in this life? What history of love can I read in this group? What has God set in motion that I can get in on?

We misunderstand and distort reality when we take ourselves as the starting point and our present situation as the basic datum. Instead of confronting the bogged-down human condition and taking charge of changing it with no time wasted, we look at divine prevenience and discern how we can get in on it at the right time, in the right way.

The cure of souls takes time to read the minutes of the previous meeting, a meeting more likely than not at which I was not present. When I engage in conversation, meet with a committee, or visit a home, I am coming in on something that has already been in process for a long time. God has been and is the central reality in that process. The biblical conviction is that God is "long beforehand with my soul." God has already taken the initiative. Like one who walks in late to a meeting, I am entering a complex situation in which God has already said decisive words and acted in decisive ways. My work is not necessarily to announce that but to discover what he is doing and live appropriately with it.

Language

In running the church I use language that is descriptive and motivational. I want people to be informed so there are no misunderstandings. And I want people to be motivated so things get done. But in the cure of souls I am far more interested in who people are and who they are becoming in Christ than I am in what they know or what they are doing. In this I soon find that neither descriptive nor motivational language helps very much.

Descriptive language is language *about* — it names what is there. It orients us in reality. It makes it possible for us to find our way in and out of intricate labyrinths. Our schools specialize in teaching us this language. Motivational language is language *for* — it uses words to get things done. Commands are issued, promises made, requests proffered. Such words get people to do things they won't do on their own initiative. The advertising industry is our most skillful practitioner of this language art.

Indispensable as these uses of language are, there is another language more essential to our humanity and far more basic to the life of faith. It is *personal* language. It uses words to express oneself, to converse, to be in relationship. This is language to and with. Love is offered and received, ideas are developed, feelings are articulated, silences are honored. This is the language we speak spontaneously as children, as lovers, as poets — and when we pray. It is also conspicuously absent when we are running a church — there is so much to say and do that there is no time left to be and no occasion, therefore, for the language of being there.

The cure of souls is a decision to work at the heart of things, where we are most ourselves and where our relationships in faith and intimacy are developed. The primary language must be, therefore, to and with, the personal language of love and prayer. The pastoral vocation does not take place primarily in a school where subjects are taught, nor in a barracks where assault forces are briefed for attacks on evil, but in a family — the place where love is learned, where birth takes place, where intimacy is deepened. The pastoral task is to use the language appropriate in this most basic aspect of our humanity — not language that describes, not language that motivates, but spontaneous language: cries and exclamations, confessions and appreciations, words the heart speaks.

We have, of course, much to teach and much to get done, but our primary task is to be. The primary language of the cure of souls, therefore, is conversation and prayer. Being a pastor means learning to use language in which personal uniqueness is enhanced and individual sanctity recognized and respected. It is a language that is unhurried, unforced, unexcited — the leisurely language of friends and lovers, which is also the language of prayer.

Problems

In running a church I solve problems. Wherever two or three are gathered together, problems develop. Egos are bruised, procedures get snarled, arrangements become confused, plans go awry. Temperaments clash. There are polity problems, marriage problems, work problems, child problems, committee problems, emotional problems. Someone has to interpret, explain, work out new plans, develop better procedures, organize, and administer. Most pastors like to do this. I know I do. It is satisfying to help make the rough places smooth.

The difficulty is that problems arrive in such a constant flow that problem solving becomes full-time work. Because it is useful and the pastor ordinarily does it well, we fail to see that the pastoral vocation has been subverted. Gabriel Marcel wrote that life is not so much a problem to be solved as a mystery to be explored. That is certainly the biblical stance: life is not something we manage to hammer together and keep in repair by our wits; it is an unfathomable gift. We are immersed in mysteries: incredible love, confounding evil, the creation, the cross, grace, God.

The secularized mind is terrorized by mysteries. Thus it makes lists, labels people, assigns roles, and solves problems. But a solved life is a reduced life. These tightly buttoned-up people never take great faith risks or make convincing love talk. They deny or ignore the mysteries and diminish human existence to what can be managed, controlled, and fixed. We live in a cult of experts who explain and solve. The vast technological apparatus around us gives the impression that there is a tool for everything if we can only afford it. Pastors cast in the role of spiritual technologists are hard put to keep that role from absorbing everything else, since there are so many things that need to be and can, in fact, be fixed.

But "there are things," wrote Marianne Moore, "that are important beyond all this fiddle." The old-time guide of souls asserts the priority of the "beyond" over "this fiddle." Who is available for this work other than pastors? A few poets, perhaps; and children, always. But children are not good guides, and most of our poets have lost interest in God. That leaves pastors as guides through the mysteries. Century after century we live with our conscience, our passions, our neighbors, and our God. Any narrower view of our relationships does not match our real humanity.

If pastors become accomplices in treating every child as a problem to be figured out, every spouse as a problem to be dealt with, every clash of wills in choir or committee as a problem to be adjudicated, we abdicate our most important work, which is directing worship in the traffic, discovering the presence of the cross in the paradoxes and chaos between Sundays, calling attention to the "splendor in the ordinary," and, most of all, teaching a life of prayer to our friends and companions in the pilgrimage.

VII

Praying with Eyes Open

Blessed are those who mourn

Flash floods of tears, torrents of them,
Erode cruel canyons, exposing
Long forgotten strata of life
Laid down in the peaceful decades:
A badlands beauty. The same sun
That decorates each day with colors
From arroyos and mesas, also shows
Every old scar and cut of lament.
Weeping washes the wounds clean
And leaves them to heal, which always
Takes an age or two. No pain
Is ugly in past tense. Under
The Mercy every hurt is a fossil
Link in the great chain of becoming.
Pick and shovel prayers often
Turn them up in valleys of death.

WRITER Annie Dillard is an exegete of creation in the same way John Calvin was an exegete of Holy Scripture. The passion and intelligence Calvin brought to Moses, Isaiah, and Paul, she brings to muskrats and mockingbirds. She reads the book of creation with the care and intensity of a skilled textual critic, probing and questioning, teasing out, with all the tools of mind and spirit at hand, the author's meaning.

Calvin was not indifferent to creation. He frequently referred to the world around us as a "theater of God's glory." He wrote of the Creator's dazzling performance in arranging the components of the cosmos. He was convinced of the wide-ranging theological significance of the doctrine of creation and knew how important the understanding of that doctrine was to protect against the gnosticism and Manichaeism that are everpresent threats to the integrity of the incarnation.

Matter is real. Flesh is good. Without a firm rooting in creation, religion is always drifting off into some kind of pious sentimentalism or sophisticated intellectualism. The task of salvation is not to refine us into pure spirits so that we will not be cumbered with this too solid flesh. We are not angels, nor are we to become angels. The Word did not become a good idea, or a numinous feeling, or a moral aspiration; the Word became flesh. It also becomes flesh. Our Lord left us a command to remember and receive him in bread and wine, in acts of eating and drinking. Things matter. The physical is holy. It is extremely significant that in the opening sentences of the Bible, God speaks a world of energy and matter into being: light, moon, stars, earth, vegetation, animals, man, woman (not love and virtue, faith and salvation, hope and judgment, though they will come soon enough). Apart from creation, covenant has no structure, no context, no rootage in reality.

Calvin knew all this, appreciated it, and taught it. But, curiously, he never seemed to have purchased a ticket to the theater, gone in, and watched the performance himself. He lived for most of his adult ministry in Geneva, Switzerland, one of the most spectacularly beautiful places on the earth. Not once does he comment on the wild thrust of the mountains into the skies. He never voices awe at the thunder of an avalanche. There is no evidence that he ever stooped to admire the gem flowers in the alpine meadows. He was not in the habit of looking up from his books and meditating before the lake loaded with sky that graced his city. He would not be distracted from this scriptural exegesis by going to the theater, even the legitimate theater of God's glory.

Aisle Seat at God's Glory

Annie Dillard has a season ticket to that theater. Day after day she takes her aisle seat and watches the performance. She is caught up in the drama of the creation. *Pilgrim at Tinker Creek* is a contemplative journal of her attendance at the theater over the course of a year. She is breathless in awe. She cries and laughs, and in turn, she is puzzled and dismayed. She is no uncritical spectator. During intermissions, she does not scruple to find fault with either writer or performance. All is not to her liking, and some scenes bring her close to revulsion. But she always returns to the action and ends up on her feet applauding, "Encore! Encore!"

> I think that the dying pray at the last not "please," but "thank you" as a guest thanks his host at the door. Falling from airplanes, the people are crying thank you, thank you, all down the air; and the cold carriages draw up for them on the rocks. Divinity is not playful. The universe was not made in jest but in solemn incomprehensible earnest. By a power that is un-

fathomably secret, and holy, and fleet. There is nothing to be done about it, but ignore it, or see. And like Billy Bray I go my way, and my left foot says "Glory," and my right foot says "Amen": in and out of Shadow Creek, upstream and down, exultant, in a daze, dancing, to the twin silver trumpets of praise.

Pilgrim at Tinker Creek was published in 1974 when Dillard was 28 years old. It won the Pulitzer Prize and brought widespread but short-lived acclaim. Nothing she has written since has commanded an equivalent attention. This is unfortunate, because American spirituality needs her.

Her unpretentiousness (the telephone call that told her she had won the Pulitzer pulled her out of a softball game in which she was playing second base) and her youthful beauty (she has long yellow hair and smiles winningly) account, perhaps, for the failure to take her seriously as a mystical theologian, which she most certainly is.

Subsequent books have developed the articulation of her spirituality. *Holy the Firm* (1977) wrestles pain to the mat in a wild, unforgettable agony. *Teaching a Stone to Talk* (1982) takes up listening posts and watchtowers from Atlantic to Pacific coasts and in both American hemispheres, contemplatively alert for the sacred voice and presence. *Living by Fiction* (1982) shifts ground slightly, searching for meaning in what people create with words (fictions), using the same critical and contemplative disciplines with which she examines what God creates with word. Her early volume of poems, *Tickets for a Prayer Wheel*, provides many of the texts and images that are developed in the prose works.

God's World at Tinker Creek

Shadow Creek. It started out as Tinker Creek, burgeoning with life: "The creator goes off on one wild, specific tangent after another, or millions simultaneously, with an exuberance that would seem to be unwarranted, and with an energy sprung from an unfathomable font. What is going on here . . . that it all flows so freely wild, like the creek, that it all surges in such a free, fringed tangle? Freedom is the world's water and weather, the world's nourishment freely given, its soil and sap: and the creator loves pizzazz."

Then one night when she was out walking, Tinker Creek vanished and Shadow Creek blocked its banks. The meaning leaked out of the creek. Imbecility replaced beauty. She praises anyway. Dark shapes intruded: the giant water bug, the dragonfly's terrible lip, the mantis's jaw, the parasites that make up 10 percent of living creatures (she calls them "the devil's tithe"). Brutality, pain, mindlessness, waste. "Shadow is the blue patch where the light doesn't hit."

It is child's play to "appreciate nature" when the sun is shining and the birds are singing. Something far more strenuous is involved when we face and deal with the cruelty and terror that the creation also deals out in spades. How we handle "the blue patch where the light doesn't hit" is the wilderness test for creation-exegesis. It is this test that pushes Dillard into a religious vocation, into holy orders.

Annie Dillard does not go in for nature appreciation; she is no gossip of the numinous. Nor is she an explainer, flattening existence into what will fit a rationalizing diagram. "These things," she says, "are not issues; they are mysteries." She is after bigger game: after meaning, after glory, after God. And she will not, as a shortcut in her pursuit, brush aside a single detail of the appalling imbecility she meets in the shadows.

Here is where she parts company with most of her contemporaries and becomes such a valuable ally in Christian pilgrimage. Avoiding the camps of neo-pagan humanists who go to the wilderness to renew their spirits, and neo-Darwinian scientists who drag specimens into the classroom to explain them, she explores the world's text with the ancient but unfashionable tools of sacrifice and prayer. She embraces spiritual disciplines in order to deal with a Creator and a creation: "Then we can at least wail the right question into the swaddling band of darkness, or, if it comes down to that, choir the proper praise."

Persons in the Middle Ages who withdrew from the traffic of the everyday to contemplate the ways of God and the mysteries of being, giving themselves to a life of sacrifice and prayer, were called anchorites (from the Greek, *anachoreo,* to withdraw to a place apart). They often lived in sheds fastened to the walls of a church. These spare shacks commonly had a world-side window through which the nun or monk received the sights and sounds of the creation as data for contemplation. These barnacle-like rooms were called anchorholds. Dillard calls her cabin on Tinker Creek an anchorhold, and plays with the word: "I think of this house clamped to the side of Tinker Creek as an anchorhold. It holds me at anchor to the rock bottom of the creek itself, and it keeps me steadied in the current, as a sea anchor does, facing the stream of light pouring down. It's a good place to live; there's a lot to think about."

She announces her exegetical agenda. First, the active mystery of creeks: "Theirs is the mystery of the continuous creation and all that providence implies: the uncertainty of vision, the horror of the fixed, the dissolution of the presence, the intricacy of beauty, the nature of perfection." And then the passive mystery of the mountains: "Theirs is the one simple mystery of creation from nothing, of matter itself, anything at all, the given. Mountains are giant, restful, absorbent. You can heave your spirit into a mountain and the mountain will keep it, folded, and not throw it back as some creeks will. The creeks are the world with all its stimulus and beauty; I live there. But the mountains are home."

It is clear now that this is not academic exegesis, weighing and measuring, sorting and parsing. This is contemplative exegesis, receiving and offering, wondering and praying. She describes her vocation as a blend of nun, thinker, and artist: "A nun lives in the fires of the spirit, a thinker lives in the bright wick of the mind, an artist lives jammed in the pool of materials. (Or, a nun lives, thoughtful and tough, in the mind, and with that special poignancy peculiar to religious, in the exile of materials; and a thinker, who would think of something, lives in the clash of materials, and in the world of spirit where all long thoughts must lead; and an artist lives in the mind, that warehouse of forms, and an artist lives, of course, in the spirit.)"

Her vocational self-understanding is most explicit in *Holy the Firm*, written in three parts as the contemplative result of three consecutive days in her life when she lived on an island in Puget Sound.

On November 18, she wakes. The world streams in through her world-side window ("I live in one room, one long wall of which is glass") and she is stunned by divinity: "Every day is a god, each day is a god, and holiness holds forth in time." She "reads" the world as a sacred script: "The world at my feet, the world through the window, is an illuminated manuscript whose leaves the wind takes, one by one, whose painted illuminations and halting words draw me, one by one, and I am dazzled in days and lost."

She seeks orientation. She draws a map of the islands visible on the horizon, fixing their locations, giving them names. She is looking around, seeing, smelling, listening: "All day long I feel created . . . created gulls pock the air, rip great curved seams in the settled air: I greet my created meal, amazed."

Even so, all is not well. She remembers a night in the mountains of Virginia when she was reading by candlelight and moths kept flying into the candle. One incinerated moth served the candle as a wick, and the flame soared through it, "a saffron-yellow flame that robed her to the ground like any immolating monk." There is pain out there. And death. There is also an immense mystery in it, something that has to do with sacrifice: the death gives light. The book she is reading is about the poet Rimbaud who burned himself out in the life of art, word-flames that illuminate the world.

Still, the day is, incredibly, fresh and full of promise. She notes that Armenians, Jews, and Catholics all salt their newborn. And all the first-offerings that Israel brought to the Lord were "a covenant of salt" preserved and savory. And the "god of today is a child, a baby new and filling the house, remarkably here in the flesh. He is day." She salts the day, as she salts her breakfast eggs, anticipating delight, exultant.

On November 19, an airplane crashes in a nearby field. She hears the sound of the crash. The pilot pulls his 7-year-old daughter from the wreckage, and as he does, a gob of ignited fuel splashes her face and burns her horribly. On November 18, she wrote, "I came here to study hard things, rock mountain and salt sea and to temper my spirit on their edges. 'Teach me thy ways, O Lord' is, like all prayers, a rash one, and one I cannot but recommend." She hadn't bargained on having to deal with a 7-year-old girl with a burnt-off face.

On November 18, God "socketed into everything that is, and that right holy." Now, on November 19, a child is in the hospital with her grieving parents at her side and "I sit at the window, chewing the bones in my wrist and pray for them. . . . Who will teach us to pray? The god of today is a glacier. We live in his shifting crevasses, unheard. The god of today is delinquent, a barn-burner, a punk with a pittance of power in a match."

What is God up to? What is real? What is illusion? She asks all the hard questions: "Has God a hand in this? Is anything firm, or is time on the loose? Did Christ descend once and for all to no purpose, in a kind of divine and kenotic suicide, or ascend once and for all, pulling his cross up after him like a rope ladder home?" And she faces the worst: "We're logrolling on a falling world, of time released from meaning and rolling loose, like one of Atalanta's golden apples, a bauble flung and forgotten, lapsed, and the gods on the lam."

She looks out of her world-side window and sees an island on the horizon that she hadn't noticed before. She names it God's Tooth.

On November 20, she walks to the store to buy the Communion wine in preparation for Sunday worship at the white frame Congregational church in the fir trees. Is there any accounting for this juxtaposition of the best and worst, this grandeur and this obscenity of the past two days? She recalls and meditates on the medieval idea that there is a created substance at the absolute base of everything, deep down "in the waxy deepness of planets, but never on the surface of planets where men can discern it; and it is in touch with the Absolute, at base . . . the name of this substance is: Holy the Firm." Everything eventually touches it. Something that touches something that touches Holy the Firm is in touch with the Absolute, with God. Islands are rooted in it, and trees, and the little girl with the slaughtered face.

Two weeks before, the little girl's parents had invited sixteen neighbors to their farm to make cider. Dillard brought her cat, and the girl played with it all afternoon. "All day long she was dressing and undressing the yellow cat, sticking it into a black dress long and full as a nun's." She and the girl resembled each other in appearance.

She names her little look-alike friend Julie Norwich. Juliana of Norwich was a fourteenth-century English nun, an anchorite, who steadily and courageously, through a suffering lifetime, looked the world's pain full in the face, and summed up her contemplation in the remarkable sentence, "And all shall be well, and all shall be well, and all manner of things shall be well." From anyone else that sentence would risk ridicule as glib gibberish, but from this nun, "thoughtful and tough . . . in the exile of materials," it is tempered truth, flexible and hard.

Dillard gives the name of the nun whose life of prayer transmuted pain to wellness to the girl whose face two weeks before was much like her own, but now puts every concept of beauty and meaning and God to hazard, and in mediatory prayer addresses her: "Held fast by love in the world like the moth in wax, your life a wick, your head on fire with prayer, held utterly, outside and in, you sleep alone, if you call that alone, you cry God." She invites her into the full goodness of life in the years ahead of her healing: "Mornings you'll whistle, full of the pleasure of days, and afternoons of this or that, and nights cry love. So live."

Then an abrupt turning, returning to her own vocation. Earlier she observed that "a life without sacrifices is abomination." Now she embraces this sacrifice, burning in a life of art and thought and prayer through the canonical hours. While "elsewhere people buy shoes," she kneels at the altar rail, holding on for dear life in the dizzying swirl of glory and brutality, and calls Julie Norwich. The last words of the book: "I'll be the nun for you. I am now."

A World of Scripture

Even though her field is creation, not Scripture exegesis, Calvin would not, I think, be displeased with Dillard's competence in Scripture. She has assimilated Scripture so thoroughly, is so saturated with its cadences and images, that it is simply at hand, unbidden, as context and metaphor for whatever she happens to be writing about. She does not, though, use Scripture to prove or document; it is not a truth she "uses" but one she lives. Her knowledge of Scripture is stored in her right brain rather than her left; nourishment for the praying imagination rather than fuel for apologetic argument. She seldom quotes Scripture; she alludes constantly. There is scarcely a page that does not contain one or several allusions, but with such nonchalance, not letting her left hand know what her right is doing, that someone without a familiarity with Scripture might never notice the biblical precept and story.

The verbal word of Scripture is the wide world within which she gives her attention to the non-verbal word of creation. The revealed world of Torah and Gospel is the spacious environment in which she works out the localized meanings of sycamore, weasels, eclipses, and sunlighted minnows. A sense of proportion develops out of her Scripture reading in which the so-called "general" revelation is subordinate to and enclosed by the "special" revelation of Scripture. She would agree, I think, with P. T. Forsyth: "It is a vast creation, but a vaster salvation."

One example: the title essay in *Teaching a Stone to Talk*, where I count seventeen allusions to Holy Scripture (not counting repeats) and three quotations. She tells the story of Larry, her neighbor on a Puget Sound island, who is trying to teach a stone to talk. He keeps the stone on his mantle, "protected by a square of untanned leather, like a canary asleep under its cloth. Larry removes the cover for the stone's lessons." The quirky story of the island crank is representational: "Nature's silence is its one remark." We are restive with the silence and are trying to raise a peep out of mute mother nature.

She finds the orienting background to the story of Larry in the story of Israel, scared witless at Sinai with its thunder and lightning, asking Moses to beg God, "Please, never speak to them directly again."

Now the entire non-human world is silent. We told God, like we tell a child who is annoying us, to shut up and go to his room. He heard our prayer. After these many centuries, we are bored and fitful with the unrelieved patter of human speech. Even our scientists, who earlier seemed to be the most determined of all to confine speech to the human, are trying to teach chimpanzees to talk, decipher the language of whales, and listen for messages from some distant star.

The island in Puget Sound on which Larry is trying to teach a stone to talk is one result of Israel's prayer; the Galapagos Islands are another. Since Darwin's time, scientists have treated the islands as a laboratory in which to find meaning in a world dissociated from the living voice of God, to study the process of evolution, to unravel the biological story of the race. Dillard goes there reading a different text, a creation text encompassed by a biblical text. She calls the Galapagos a "kind of metaphysics laboratory." She might as well have called them a prayer laboratory.

The sea lion is the most popular resident of the Galapagos, gregarious and graceful, welcoming and sportive, "engaged in full-time play." Visitors joke that when they "come back" they would like to come as a sea lion. "The sea lion game looked unbeatable." After long reflection and another visit to the island, she made a different choice: the palo santo tree. She had hardly noticed them on her first visit. The trees were thin, pale, wispy miles of them, half dead, the stands looking like blasted orchards. She chose the palo santo because even though "the silence is all there is," it is not a silence of absence but of presence. It is not a sterile silence, but a pregnant silence. The non-human silence is not because there is nothing to say but because, in disobedience or unbelief or sheer terror, we asked God not to speak and God heard our prayer. But though unspeaking, God is still there. What is needed from us is witness. The palo santo is a metaphor for witness.

The premier biblical witness, John the Baptist, said, "He must increase, but I must decrease." The witness does not call attention to itself; what it points to is more important. Being takes precedence over using, explaining, possessing. The witness points, mute, so as not to interfere with the sound of silence: the palo santos "interest me as emblems of the muteness of the human stance in relation to all that is not human. I see us all as palo santo trees, holy sticks, together watching all that we watch, and growing in silence."

Witness is the key word in all this. It is an important biblical word in frequent contemporary use. It is a modest word saying what is there, honestly testifying to exactly what we see, what we hear. But when we enlist in a cause, it is almost impossible to do it right: we embellish, we fill in the blanks, we varnish the dull passages, we gild the lily just a little to hold the attention of our auditors. Sea lion stuff. Important things are at stake — God, salvation — and we want so much to involve outsiders in these awesome realities that we leave the humble ground of witness and use our words to influence and motivate, to advertise and publicize. Then we are no longer witnesses, but lawyers arguing the case, not always with scrupulous attention to detail. After all, life and death issues are before the jury.

Dillard returns us to the spare, simple, modest role of

witness. We live in a time when the voice of God has been extinguished in the creation. We want the stones to talk, the heavens to declare the glory of God, but "the very holy mountains are keeping mum. We doused the burning bush and cannot rekindle it; we are lighting matches in vain under every green tree. Did the wind used to cry, and the hills shout forth praise? Now speech has perished from among the lifeless things of earth, and living things say very little to very few."

Our necessary and proper work in such a world is witness like the palo santo trees.

The World in a Church

The American writers with whom Dillard is often grouped — Henry Thoreau, Waldo Emerson, John Muir — didn't go to church. They distanced themselves from what they saw as the shabbiness and hypocrisy of institutional religion and opted for the pine purity of forest cathedrals. Emily Dickinson gave them their text: "Some worship God by going to church/I worship him staying at home/with a bobolink for a chorister/and an orchard for a throne." Their numerous progeny spend Sunday mornings on birdwatching field trips and Sierra Club walks. Annie Dillard goes to church: "I know only enough of God to want to worship him, by any means ready to hand. . . . There is one church here, so I go to it." It doesn't matter that it is out of fashion, she goes anyway: "On a big Sunday there might be twenty of us there; often I am the only person under sixty, and feel as though I'm on an archaeological tour of Soviet Russia."

It is unfashionable because it is ridiculous. How can searchers after God and seekers after beauty stomach the "dancing bear act" that is staged in Christian churches, Protestant and Catholic alike, week after week? Dillard, cheerfully and matter-of-factly, goes anyway. Her tour de force on worship, "An Expedition to The Pole," provides the image and rationale. Wherever we go, to the pole or the church, "there seems to be only one business at hand: that of finding workable compromises between the sublimity of our ideas and the absurdity of the fact of us."

In *Pilgrim,* she wrote, "These northings drew me, present northings, past northings, the thought of northings. In the literature of polar exploration, the talk is of northing. An explorer might scrawl in his tattered journal, 'Latitude 82 + 15' N. We accomplished 20 miles of northing today, in spite of the shifting pack.' Shall I go northing? My legs are long." She describes the parallel goals. The pole of Relative Inaccessibility is "that imaginary point on the Arctic Ocean farthest from land in any direction." Reading the accounts of polar explorers, one is impressed that at root they were seeking the sublime. "Simplicity and purity attracted them; they set out to perform clear tasks in uncontaminated lands. . . . They praised the land's spare beauty as if it were a moral or a spiritual quality: 'icy halls of cold sublimity,' 'lofty peaks perfectly covered with eternal snow.'" That is geography. There is an equivalent pole in worship: "the Absolute is the pole of Relative Inaccessibility located in metaphysics. After all, one of the few things we know about the Absolute is that it is relatively inaccessible. It is the point of spirit farthest from every accessible point of spirit in all directions. Like the others, it is a pole of the Most Trouble. It is also, I take this as a given, the pole of great price."

She quotes Fridtjof Nansen on polar exploration, referring to "the great adventure of the ice, deep and pure as infinity . . . the eternal round of the universe and its eternal death" and notes that everywhere "polar prose evokes these absolutes, these ideas of 'eternity' and 'perfection' as if they were some

81

perfectly visible part of the landscape." And she quotes Pope Gregory, who calls us to Christian worship "to attain to somewhat of the unencompassed light, by stealth, and scantily."

She tells the comic-tragic stories of polar explorers who "despite the purity of their conceptions . . . manhauled their humanity to the poles." The Franklin Expedition in 1845, with 138 officers and men, carried a "1,200 volume library, a handorgan playing fifty tunes, china place settings for officers and men, cutglass wine goblets, sterling silver flatware, and no special clothing for the Arctic, only the uniforms of Her Majesty's Navy." It was a noble enterprise, and they were nobly dressed for it. They all died. Their corpses were found with pieces of backgammon board and a great deal of table silver engraved with officers' initials and family crests. Dignity was all.

Sir Robert Falcon Scott had a different kind of dignity: he thought the purity of polar search dictated a purity of effort unaided by dogs or companions. He also died. "There is no such thing as a solitary polar explorer, fine as the conception is." Some of the most moving documents of polar writing, expressing his lofty sentiments, his purity and dignity and self-control, were found under his frozen carcass.

The explorers who made it weren't so fussy. They abandoned their roles, their privileges, their preconceived notions, and adapted to the conditions of pack ice and glaciers in the light-drenched land.

Annie Dillard going to worship — "a kind of northing is what I wish to accomplish, a single-minded trek toward that place" — faces equivalent difficulties. Her experiences in the church's worship are interweaved with commentary on polar explorations. The amateurism is distressing: "A high school stage play is more polished than this service we have been rehearsing since the year one. In two thousand years we have not worked out the kinks."

The attempts to be relevant are laughable: "I have over-come a fiercely anti-Catholic upbringing in order to attend Mass simply and solely to escape Protestant guitars."

The blithe ignorance is frightening: "Why do we people in churches seem like cheerful, brainless tourists on a packaged tour of the Absolute? . . . On the whole, I do not find Christians, outside the catacombs, sufficiently sensible of conditions. Does anyone have the foggiest idea what sort of power we so blithely invoke? Or, as I suspect, does not one believe a word of it? The churches are children playing on the floor with their chemistry sets, mixing up a batch of TNT to kill a Sunday morning. It is madness to wear ladies' straw hats and velvet hats to church; we should all be wearing crash helmets. Ushers should issue life preservers and signal flares: they should lash us to our pews." Explorers unmindful of "conditions" died. Why don't similarly unprepared worshipers perish on the spot?

Never mind. She sheds her dignity, sloughs off schooling and scruples, abandons propriety. "I would rather, I think, undergo the famous dark night of the soul than encounter in church the dread hootenanny, but these purely personal preferences are of no account, and maladaptive to boot." So she manhauls her humanity to her pew, gives up her personal dignity, and throws in her lot with random people. She realizes that one can no more go to God alone than go to the pole alone. She further realizes that even though the goal is pure, the people are not pure, and if we want to go to the Land we must go with the people, even when they are playing banjos, singing stupid songs, and giving vacuous sermons. "How often have I mounted this same expedition, has my absurd barque set out half-caulked for the pole?"

So she worships. Weekly she sets out for the pole of Relative Inaccessibility, "where the twin oceans of beauty and horror meet." Dignity and culture abandoned, silence and solitude abandoned, she joins the motley sublime/ludicrous people who show up in polar expeditions and church congregations. "Week after week we witness the same miracle: that God, for reasons unfathomable, refrains from blowing our dancing bear act to smithereens. Week after week, Christ washes the disciples' dirty feet, handles their very toes, and repeats, 'It is all right, believe it or not, to be people.'"

The spiritualities involved in going to the pole and to church are essentially the same. Dillard embraces both. And she deals with the hard things in both ventures, the absurd vanities in the explorers and the embarrassing shabbiness in the worshipers, with immense charity. She is blessedly free, whether in the wilderness or at worship, of sentimentalism and snobbery (the twin sins of touristy aesthetes). She is as accepting of absurdities in Christian worship as she is of absurdities in polar exploration. She is saying, I think, that we have put up with nature sentimentalism and liturgical snobbery long enough. If there are difficulties in going to church, they are no greater than those encountered in going to the pole. As she says, "Nobody said things were going to be easy."

Prayer: Eyes Open or Shut?

There are two great mystical traditions in the life of prayer, sometimes labeled kataphatic and apophatic. Kataphatic prayer uses icons, symbols, ritual, incense; the creation is the way to the Creator. Apophatic prayer attempts emptiness; the creature distracts from the Creator, and so the mind is systematically emptied of idea, image, sensation until there is only the simplicity of being. Kataphatic prayer is "praying with your eyes open"; apophatic prayer is "praying with your eyes shut."

At our balanced best, the two traditions intermingle, mix,

and cross-fertilize. But we are not always at our best. The Western church is heavily skewed on the side of the apophatic. The rubric for prayer when I was a child was, "Fold your hands, bow your head, shut your eyes, and we'll pray." My early training carries over into my adult practice. Most of my praying still is with my eyes shut. I need balancing.

Annie Dillard prays differently: Spread out your hands, lift your head, open your eyes, and we'll pray. "It is still the first week in January, and I've got great plans. I've been thinking about seeing. There are lots of things to see, unwrapped gifts and free surprises." We start out with her on what we suppose will be no more than a walk through the woods. It is not long before we find ourselves in the company of saints and monks, enlisted in the kind of contemplative seeing "requiring a lifetime of dedicated struggle."

She gets us into the theater that Calvin told us about, and we find ourselves in the solid biblical companionship of psalmists and prophets who watched the "hills skip like lambs" and heard the "trees clap their hands," alert to God everywhere, in everything, praising, praying with our eyes open: "I leap to my feet; I cheer and cheer."

VIII

First Language

Blessed are the meek

Moses, by turns raging and afraid,
Was meek under the thunderhead whiteness,
The glorious opacity of cloudy pillar.
Each cloud is meek, buffeted by winds
It changes shape but never loses
Being: not quite liquid, hardly
Solid, in medias res. Like me.
Yielding to the gusting spirit
All become what ministering angels
Command: sign, promise, portent.
Vigorous in image and color, oh, colors
Of earth pigments mixed with sun
Make hues that raise praises at dusk,
At dawn, collect storms, release
Rain, filter sun in arranged
And weather measured shadows.
Sunpatches.

I ENTERED into my pastoral calling with a great charge of educational zest. My mind fairly tumbled with stories and facts, insights and perspectives, that give the life of faith such richness and texture. I had been on an exuberant foray into the country of Scripture and theology in my years of study and was eager to take others on safari with me. I knew I could rescue the Arian controversy from textbook dullness and present the decipherment of Ugaritic in such ways that would enhance appreciation for the subtle elegances of biblical language and story. I couldn't wait to get started.

No place seemed to me better suited to such endeavors than the Christian congregation. It was far better than any school. People came to church not because they had to but because they willed it. They brought a level of motivation to learning that was far higher than in any academic assembly. Nobody was there just to get a grade or a diploma. They came together in a community of faith wanting to love the Lord with both mind and heart. And they had called me to help them do it.

So I taught. I taught from pulpit and lectern. I taught in home and classroom. I taught adults and youth and children. I formed special groups, arranged mini-courses, conducted seminars. The ones who loitered and held back I promoted and persuaded. I had people studying Isaiah and Mark, Reformation theology and Old Testament archaeology, who hadn't used their minds in a disciplined way since they got their high school diplomas or college degrees. I didn't, of course, get everyone, but by and large I was not disappointed. I had a wonderful time.

What Is My Educational Task?

After a few years of this, I noticed how different my teaching was from that of early generations of pastors. My secularized schooling had shaped my educational outlook into something with hardly any recognizable continuities with most of the church's history. I had come into the parish seeing its great potential as a learning center, a kind of mini-university in which I was the resident professor.

And then one day, in a kind of shock of recognition, I saw that it was in fact a worship center. I wasn't prepared for this. Nearly all my preparation for being a pastor had taken place in a classroom, with chapels and sanctuaries ancillary to it. But these people I was now living with were coming, with centuries of validating precedence, not to get facts on the Philistines and Pharisees but to pray. They were hungering to grow in Christ, not bone up for an examination in dogmatics. I began to comprehend the obvious: that the central and shaping language of the church's life has always been its prayer language.

Out of that recognition a conviction grew: that my primary educational task as pastor was to teach people to pray. I did not abandon, and will not abandon, the task of teaching about the faith, teaching the content of the gospel, the historical backgrounds of biblical writings, the history of God's people. I have no patience with and will not knowingly give comfort to obscurantist or anti-intellectual tendencies in the church. But there is an educational task entrusted to pastors that is very different from that assigned to professors. The educational approaches in all the schools I attended conspired to ignore the wisdom of the ancient spiritual leaders who trained people in the disciplines of attending to God, forming the inner life so that it was adequate to the reception of truth, not just the acquisition of facts. The more I worked with people at or near the centers of their lives where God and the human, faith and the absurd, love and indifference were tangled in daily traffic jams, the less it seemed that the way I had been going about teaching made much difference, and the more that teaching them to pray did.

Help Available

It is not easy to keep this conviction in focus, for the society in which I live sees education primarily as information retrieval. But there is help available.

Most of mine came from making friends with some ancestors long dead. Gregory of Nyssa and Teresa of Avila got me started. I took these masters as my mentors. They expanded my concept of prayer and introduced me into the comprehensive and imaginative and vigorous language of prayer. They convinced me that teaching people to pray was my best work.

Other help has come from an unexpected quarter among my contemporaries, the philosophers of language (especially Ludwig Wittgenstein and Eugen Rosenstock-Huessy). Under their influence I came to be in awe of the way language works and to realize the immense mysteries that surround speech. I started paying attention to the way I used language both as a person and as a pastor. These philosophers gave me a compass that showed me the way to recover the kind of language that seemed more or less native to earlier generations in the faith, the language that was required if I were to keep faith with my pastoral vocation and teach people to pray.

I have reduced and simplified and summarized what I have learned in these respects into a kind of rough language map showing three sections: Language I, Language II, and Language III.

Three Types of Language

Language I is the language of intimacy and relationship. It is the first language we learn. Initially, it is not articulate speech. The language that passes between parent and infant is incredibly rich in meaning but less than impressive in content. The coos and cries of the infant do not parse. The nonsense syllables of the parent have no dictionary definitions. But in the exchange of gurgles and out-of-tune hums, trust develops. Parent whispers transmute infant screams into grunts of hope. The cornerstone words in this language are names, or pet names: mama, papa. For all its limited vocabulary and butchered syntax, it seems more than adequate to bring into expression the realities of a complex and profound love. Language I is primary language, the basic language for expressing and developing the human condition.

Language II is the language of information. As we grow, we find this marvelous world of things surrounding us, and everything has a name: rock, water, doll, bottle. Gradually, through the acquisition of language, we are oriented in a world of objects. Beyond the relational intimacy with persons with which we begin, we find our way in an objective environment of trees and fire engines and weather. Day after day words are added. Things named are no longer strange but familiar. We make friends with the world. We learn to speak in sentences, making connections. The world is wonderfully various and our language enables us to account for it, recognizing what is there and how it is put together. Language II is the major language used in schools.

Language III is the language of motivation. We discover early on that words have the power to make things happen, to bring something out of nothing, to move inert figures into purposive action. An infant wail brings food and a dry diaper. A parental command arrests a childish tantrum. No physical force is involved. No material causation is visible. Just a word: stop, go, shut up, speak up, eat everything on your plate. We are moved by language and use it to move others. Children acquire a surprising proficiency in this language, moving people much bigger and more intelligent than themselves to strenuous activity (and often against both the inclination and better judgment of these people). Language III is the predominant language of advertising and politics.

Languages II and III are, clearly, the ascendant languages of our culture. Informational language (II) and motivational language (III) dominate our society. We are well schooled in language that describes the world in which we live. We are well trained in language that moves people to buy and join and vote. Meanwhile Language I, the language of intimacy, the language that develops relationships of trust and hope and understanding, languishes. Once we are clear of the cradle, we find less and less occasion to use it. There are short-lived recoveries of Language I in adolescence when we fall in love and spend endless hours talking on the telephone using words that eavesdroppers would characterize as gibberish. In romantic love, we find that it is the only language adequate to the reality of our passions. When we are new parents, we relearn the basic language and use it for a while. A few people never quit using it — a few lovers, some poets, the saints — but most let it slide.

Converting Language

When I first started listening to language with these discriminations, I realized how thoroughly culture-conditioned I was. Talk about being conformed to this world! My use of language in the community of faith was a mirror image of the culture: a lot of information, a lot of publicity, not much intimacy. My ministry was voiced almost entirely in the language of description and of persuasion — telling what was there, urging what could be. I was a great explainer. I was a pretty good exhorter. I was duplicating in the church what I had learned in my thoroughly secularized schools and sales-saturated society, but I wasn't giving people much help in developing and using the language that was basic to both their humanity and their faith, the language of love and prayer.

But this is my basic work: on the one hand to proclaim the word of God that is personal — God addressing us in love, inviting us into a life of trust in him; on the other hand to guide and encourage an answering word that is likewise personal — to speak in the first person to the second person, I to Thou, and avoid third-person commentary as much as possible. This is my essential educational task: to develop and draw out into articulateness this personal word, to teach people to pray. Prayer is Language I. It is not language *about* God or the faith; it is not language in the service *of* God and the faith; it is language *to* and *with* God in faith.

I remembered a long-forgotten sentence by George Arthur Buttrick, a preacher under whom I sat for a year of Sunday morning sermons while in seminary: "Pastors think people come to church to hear sermons. They don't; they come to pray and to learn to pray." I remembered Anselm's critical transition from talking about God to talking to God. He had written his *Monologion,* setting forth the proofs of God's existence with great brilliance and power. It is one of the stellar theological achievements in the West. Then he realized that however many right things he had said about God, he had said them all in the wrong language. He re-wrote it all in a *Proslogion,* converting his Language II into Language I: first-person address, an answer to God, a personal conversation with the personal God. The *Proslogion* is theology as prayer.

If the primary preaching task of the pastor is the conversion of lives, the primary teaching task is the conversion of language. I haven't quit using the languages of information and motivation, nor will I. Competency in all languages is necessary in this life of faith that draws all levels of existence into the service and glory of God. But I have determined that the language in which I must be most practiced and for which I have a primary responsibility for teaching proficiency in others is Language I, the language of relationship, the language of prayer — to get as much language as possible into the speech of love and response and intimacy.

"Abba! Father!"

IX

Is Growth a Decision?

**Blessed are those who hunger
and thirst after righteousness**

*Unfeathered unbelief would fall
Through the layered fullness of thermal
Updrafts like a rock; this red-tailed
Hawk drifts and slides, unhurried
Though hungry, lazily scornful
Of easy meals off carrion junk,
Expertly waiting elusive provisioned
Prey: a visible emptiness
Above an invisible plenitude.
The sun paints the Japanese
Fantail copper, etching
Feathers against the big sky
To my eye's delight, and blesses
The better-sighted bird with a shaft
Of light that targets a rattler
In a Genesis-destined death.*

THE PEOPLE with whom I grew up talked a lot about "breaking the will." The task of every devout parent was to "break the will" of the child. I don't remember ever hearing it used by adults on one another, but that may be a more or less willful defect in my memory.

The assumption underlying this linchpin in the program for Christian development in our church was, apparently, that the will, especially a child's will, is contrary to God's will. A broken will presumably left one open to the free play of God's will.

Fifty years later, I recall my now grown-up friends who were enrolled in this school of childhood spirituality and along with me got their wills broken with regularity. By my observations, we all seem to have passed through the decades every bit as pigheaded and stiff-necked as any of our uncircumcised Philistine companions who never went to church, or at least not to churches that specialized in breaking the wills of little kids. Apparently broken wills mend the same way that broken arms and legs do, stronger at the line of fracture.

At the same time, I also recall a lot of emphasis in our church on "making a decision for the Lord," and exercising my willpower in saying no to the temptations that surrounded me in school and neighborhood. I had many occasions to do that, making repeated decisions for Christ as evangelists and pastors took turns at sowing doubts about the validity of my last decision and urging me to do it again. My schoolmates provided daily practice in exercising my nay-saying willpower as they offered up the attractions of world, flesh, and devil.

Hung on the wall of my room at home was a framed picture of a three-masted ship with wind-filled sails on a blue background. Under the picture was a verse:

Ships sail East, and ships sail West,
while the selfsame breezes blow.

> It's the set of the sail, and not the gale
> that determines the way they go.

I could see the picture and verse as I laid in bed. I learned
the use of the rudder and how to tack before the wind by
pondering that rectangle of blue. The doggerel embedded itself
in me. The picture became a kind of mandala that gathered
the energies of will — my childhood yea-saying at the altar calls
and nay-saying on the playgrounds — into visual form. The
verse took on the force of a mantra. Together, picture and verse
confirmed with the force of Scripture the capacity of my will
to determine the direction of my life, which I never doubted
was a life following Christ.

These two approaches to the will, breaking it and exercising it, existed alongside each other through my childhood and
youth. It never occurred to me to see them in contradiction,
canceling each other out. Nor does it now. But in adulthood I
did become puzzled by their apparent dissonance.

I set off in search of counsel that had more wisdom than
the simplistic slogan (break the will) and doggerel verse (It's
the set of the sail) that seemed to serve well enough as I grew
up.

Human Will and God's Will

I found, early in my search, that I was not the first to be puzzled.
I found a large company of men and women scratching their
heads over these matters. I found myself, in fact, in the middle
of a centuries-long discussion that is still in progress. Hamlet's
question, *To be or not to be?* is not ours. Being is not in question.
Willing is. *To will or not to will?*

In a gospel of divine grace, what place does the human

will play? In a world in which God's will initiates everything, does our will only get in the way? In a creation brought into being by God's will and in a salvation executed by Christ's will, what is left for a human will?

On the positive side, willing is the core of my being. If my will is broken, am I myself? Am I complete? Am I not a cripple, limping along on a crutch? The capacity to make a decision, to direct life, to exercise freedom is the very thing that needs developing if I am to make a decision for Christ — which I grew up believing to be the most important act of will there is. I still believe that.

Without an exercised will, I am a dishrag, limp in a dirty sink. If I am anemic in will, the imperatives that are staccato stabs throughout the gospel message (come, follow, rise, love) sink into marshmallow piety without drawing one drop of red blood.

But the moment I begin exercising my will, I find that I have put a fox in charge of the chicken coop. That is the negative side. The poor Rhode Island Reds that had been laying so well — humility, trust, mercy, patience, kindness, hope — are doomed. It is a heady experience to find that I am in charge of my life and, although I wouldn't think of dismissing God, no longer have the need to depend wimpily upon him.

My will is my glory; it is also what gives me the most trouble. There is something deeply flawed in me that separates me from the God who wills my salvation; that "something" seems to be located in and around my will. I ponder St. Paul, "I do not understand my own actions. For I do not do what I want, but I do the very thing I hate" (Rom. 7:15), and I pray with my Lord, "Not as I will but as thou wilt" (Matt. 26:39).

To will or not to will, that is the question.

Searching the Intersection

I prayed and pondered. I asked questions and read books. I looked around. It wasn't long before I realized I had set up shop at heavily trafficked crossroads.

Not only were God and my consequent spirituality at issue, but nearly everything that was distinctively human about me — the way I worked, the way I talked, the way I loved. Standing in the presence of these mysteries — work, language, love — I found insights developing and experiences occurring that were convergent with the greatest mystery: God and my relationship to him in prayer and belief and obedience.

The question at the heart of the intersection of God's will and human wills is apparently at the heart of everything. The relation of God's will and my will is not a specialized religious question; it is *the* question. The way we answer it shapes our humanity in every dimension.

...tention to what was happening in my ...ogy — beyond, that is, getting fed and ...ssue of will was involved, and in a way ...ple. Always other wills were involved ...ple alternatives of either asserting my ...nother will.

...experience where I have paid particular ...o all: we all work; we all use language; ...d (even if only intermittently).

Work: Negative Capability

I entered the world of work at an early age in my father's butcher shop. This was a privileged world, this adult world of work, and when I was working in it I was, in my own mind anyway, an adult. When I was 5 years old, my mother made me a white butcher's apron. Every year, as I grew, she made another to size. To this day, I picture the linen ephod that Hannah made for the boy Samuel cut on the pattern of, and from similar material as, my butcher's apron.

I was started out on easy jobs of sweeping and cleaning display windows. I graduated to grinding hamburger. One of the men would pick me up and stand me on an upended orange crate before the big, red Hobart meat grinder, and I in my linen ephod would push the chunks of beef into its maw. The day I was trusted with a knife and taught to respect it and keep it sharp, I knew adulthood was just around the corner.

"That knife has a will of its own," old Eddie Nordham, one of my dad's butchers, used to say to me. "Get to know your knife." If I cut myself, he would blame me not for carelessness but for ignorance — I didn't "know" my knife.

I also learned that a beef carcass has a will of its own — it is not just an inert mass of meat and gristle and bone, but has character and joints, texture and grain. Carving a quarter of beef into roasts and steaks was not a matter of imposing my knife-fortified will on dumb matter, but respectfully and reverently entering into the reality of the material.

"Hackers" was my father's contemptuous label for butchers who ignorantly imposed their wills on the meat. They didn't take into account the subtle differences between pork and beef. They used knives and cleavers inappropriately and didn't keep them sharp. They were bullies forcing their wills on slabs of bacon and hind quarters of beef. The results were unattractive and uneconomical. They commonly left a mess behind that the rest of us had to clean up.

Real work always includes a respect for the material at hand. The material can be a pork loin, or a mahogany plank, or a lump of clay, or the will of God, but when the work is done well there is a kind of submission of will to the conditions at hand, a cultivation of humility. It is a noticeable feature in all skilled workers — woodworkers, potters, poets, and prayers. I learned it in the butcher shop.

"Negative capability" is the phrase the poet John Keats coined to refer to this experience in work. He was impressed by William Shakespeare's work in making such a variety of characters in his plays, none of which seemed to be a projection of Shakespeare's ego. Each had an independent life of his or her own. Keats wrote, "A poet has no Identity . . . he is continually . . . filling some other Body." He believed that the only way real creative will matured was in a person who was not hell-bent on imposing his or her will on another person or thing but "was capable of being in uncertainties, mysteries, doubts, without any irritable searching after fact and reason." Interesting: Shakespeare, the poet from whom we know the most about people, is the poet about whom we know next to nothing.

Adolescents are workers bent on self-expression. The results are maudlin. Simpering songs. Sprawling poems. Banal letters. Bombastic reforms. Bursts of energy that run out of gas (the self tank doesn't hold that much fuel) and litter house and neighborhood with unfinished models, friendships, and projects. The adolescent, excited at finding the wonderful Self, supposes that life now consists in expressing it for the edification of all others. Most of us are bored.

Real work, whether it involves making babies or poems, hamburger or holiness, is not self-expression, but its very opposite. Real workers, skilled workers, practice negative capability — the suppression of self so that the work can take place on its own. St. John the Baptist's "I must decrease, but he must increase" is embedded in all good work. When we work well, our tastes, experiences, and values are held in check so that the nature of the material or the person or the process or our God is as little adulterated or compromised by our ego as possible. The worker in the work is a self-effacing servant. If the worker shows off in his or her work, the work is ruined and becomes bad work — a projection of ego, an indulgence of self.

St. Paul's description of Jesus, "emptied himself" (Phil. 2:7), is often cited as the center point in the work of Incarnation, the making of our salvation. *Kenosis*. Emptying is prelude to filling. The Son of God empties himself of prerogative, of divine rights, of status and reputation, in order to be the one whom God uses to fill up creation and creatures with the glory of salvation. A bucket, no matter what wonderful things it contains, is of no use for the next task at hand until it is emptied. Negative capability.

I now see that all the jobs I have ever been given have been apprenticeships in the work of God. What I experience in kitchen, bedroom, workshop, athletic arena, studio, and sanctuary trains me in the subtleties of negative capability. I will to not will what I am already good at in order that what is more than me and beyond me, the will of God, can come into existence in my willing work.

Language: The Middle Voice

Five hundred miles further west and ten years later, another strand of experience entered my life, sat alongside the butcher's knife for a few years, and then converged with it to provide insight into the nature of the praying will.

For four years, minus vacations, I made a daily descent into a basement room in MacMillan Hall at the foot of Queen Anne Hill in Seattle. Light came uncertainly through Venetian blinds from shallow windows high in the walls. I was learning Greek. I puzzled over many strange things those years under the soft-spoken patience of my professor, Dr. Winifred Weter.

I puzzled longest over the middle voice. It was a small class, five of us I think, and I was the last to get it. In a class that size slowness is conspicuous, and I was unhappy with my growing reputation as the class tortoise. Then one day, a winter afternoon of Seattle drizzle, the room filled with light, or at least my corner of it did. We were about two-thirds of the way through Xenophon's *Anabasis* when I got the hang of the mysterious middle voice.

At the time I thought only that I had nailed down an elusive piece of Greek grammar. Years later I realized that I had grasped a large dimension of being and a way of prayer. I was the slowest in my class but by no means the only person to have difficulty coming to terms with the middle voice. Active and passive voices I understood, but middle was a new kid on the block. When I speak in the active voice, I initiate an action that goes someplace else: "I counsel my friend." When I speak in the passive voice, I receive the action that another initiates: "I am counseled by my friend." When I speak in the middle voice, I actively participate in the results of an action that another initiates: "I take counsel." Most of our speech is divided between active and passive; either I act or I am acted upon. But there are moments, and they are those in which we are most distinctively human, when such a contrast is not satisfactory: two wills operate, neither to the exclusion of the other, neither canceling out the other, each respecting the other.

My grammar book said, "The middle voice is that use of the verb which describes the subjects as participating in the results of the action." I read that now, and it reads like a description of Christian prayer — "the subject as participating in the results of the action." I do not control the action; that is a pagan concept of prayer, putting the gods to work by my incantations or rituals. I am not controlled by the action; that is a Hindu concept of prayer in which I slump passively into the impersonal and fated will of gods and goddesses. I enter into the action begun by another, my creating and saving Lord, and find myself participating in the results of the action. I neither do it, nor have it done to me; I will to participate in what is willed.

Prayer and spirituality feature participation, the complex participation of God and the human, his will and our wills. We do not abandon ourselves to the stream of grace and drown in the ocean of love, losing identity. We do not pull the strings that activate God's operations in our lives, subjecting God to our assertive identity. We neither manipulate God (active voice) nor are manipulated by God (passive voice). We are involved in the action and participate in its results but do not control or define it (middle voice). Prayer takes place in the middle voice.

Now comes a most fascinating sentence in my grammar: "Nothing is more certain than that the parent language of our family possessed no passive, but only active and middle, the latter originally equal with the former in prominence, though unrepresented now in any language, save by forms which have lost all distinction of meaning." No passive! Think of it: back at the origins of our language, there was no way to express an action in which I was not somehow, in some way, involved as a participant.

But the farther we travel from Eden, the less use we have for the middle voice, until it finally atrophies for lack of use. We either take charge of our own destinies (active voice) or let others take charge and slip into animal passivity before forces too great for us (passive voice). The gospel restores the middle voice. We learn to live with praying-willing involvement in an action that we do not originate. We become subjects in an action in which we are personally involved. In the middle voice objects take second place to subjects — everyone and everything becomes subject.

Eden pride and disobedience delete the middle and reduce us to two voices, active and passive. We end up taking sides. We don't have enough (or any!) verbal experience in this third voice, this voice that is fine-tuned to the exquisitely and uniquely human venture of entering into and responding to God. But no friendship, no love affair, no marriage can exist with only active and passive voices. Something else is required, a mode of willingness that radiates into a thousand subtleties of participation and intimacy, trust and forgiveness and grace.

At our human and Christian best we are not fascists barking our orders to God and his creatures. At our human and Christian best we are not quietists dumbly submissive before fate. At our human and Christian best we pray in the middle voice at the center between active and passive, drawing from them as we have need and occasion but always uniquely and artistically ourselves, creatures adoring God and being graced by him, "participating in the results of the action."

And to think I got my start in learning this during that long winter of Seattle rain while reading Xenophon!

Love: Willed Passivity

After another decade and a few years into marriage, I was surprised to find myself at the center of what has turned out to be the richest experience yet in my will and God's will. I had supposed when I entered marriage that it was mostly about sexuality, domesticity, companionship, and children. The surprise was that I was in a graduate school for spirituality —

prayer and God — with daily assignments and frequent exams in matters of the will.

(What I have learned in marriage can be just as well, maybe better, learned in friendship. The unmarried have just as much experience to work with as the married. But since my primary experience has been in marriage, I will write of it.)

It goes without saying that in marriage two wills are in operation at the same time. Sometimes, and especially in the early months of marriage, the two wills are spontaneously congruent and experienced as one. But as time goes by and early ecstasies are succeeded by routines and demands, what was experienced as a gift must be developed as an art.

The art is willed passivity. The phrase sounds self-contradictory, but it is not, and converges with what I started out learning in my father's butcher shop and continued in Professor Weter's Greek class.

Learning the art of willed passivity begins with appreciating the large and creative part passivity plays in our lives. By far the largest part of our life is experienced in the mode of passivity. Life is undergone. We receive. We enter into what is already there. Our genetic system, the atmosphere, the food chain, our parents, the dog — they are there, in place, before we exercise our will.

"Eighty percent of life," says Woody Allen, "is just showing up." Nothing we do by the exercise of our wills will ever come close to approximating what is done to us by other wills. Our lives enter into what is already done; most of life is not what we do but what is done to us. If we deny or avoid these passivities, we live in a very small world. The world of our activities is a puny enterprise; the world of our passivities is a vast cosmos. We experience as happening to us weather, our bodies, our parents, much of our government, the landscape, much of our education.

But there are different ways of being passive: there is an indolent, inattentive passivity that approximates the existence of a slug; and there is a willed and attentive passivity that is something more like worship.

St. Paul's famous "Wives, be subject to your husbands. Husbands, love your wives, as Christ loved the church and gave himself up for her" (Eph. 5:22–25) sets down the parallel operations of willed passivity.

An earlier sentence establishes the necessary context, apart from which the dual instructions can only be misunderstood. The sentence is: "Be subject to one another out of reverence for Christ" (Eph. 5:21).

Reverence is the operative word — *en phobo Christou* — awed, worshipful attentiveness, ready to respond in love and adoration. We do not learn our relationship with God out of a cocksure, arrogant knowledge of exactly what God wants (which then launches us into a vigorous clean-up campaign of the world on his behalf, in the course of which we shout orders up at him, bossing him around so that he can assist us in accomplishing his will). Nor do we cower before him in a scrupulous anxiety that fears offending him, only venturing a word or an action when explicitly commanded and at all other times worrying endlessly of what we might have done to offend him.

No, gospel reverence, Christ reverence, spouse reverence is a vigorous (but by no means presumptuous) bold freedom, full of spontaneous energy. This is the contextual atmosphere in which we find ourselves loved and loving before God.

We are more than ready to bow down before Christ unafraid that we will be tyrannized, for Christ has already laid down his life for us on the cross, pouring himself out and holding nothing back. Willed passivity.

St. Paul teaches husbands and wives how their wills can become the means for love and not the weapons of war. He counsels willed passivity in both marriage partners as an analogy of Christ's willingness to be sacrificed. Love is defined by a willingness to give up my will ("not my will but thine be done"), a voluntary crucifixion.

Marriage provides extensive experience in the possibilities of willed passivity. We find ourselves in daily relationship with a complex reality we did not make — this *person* with functioning heart and kidneys, with glorious (and not so glorious) emotions, capable of interesting us profoundly one minute and then boring us insufferably the next, and most mysterious of all, with a will, the freedom to choose and direct and intend a shared life intimacy.

And all the time I am also all those things, also with a will. When we are doing it right, and not always knowing how we are doing it right, the two wills enhance and glorify each other. We learn soon that love does not develop when we impose our will on the other, but only when we enter into sensitive responsiveness to the will of the other, what I am calling willed passivity. If the operation is mutual, which it sometimes is, a great love is the consequence. The high failure rate in marriage is the sad statistical witness to the difficulties involved. We would rather operate as activists in our love, commanding our beloved in actions that please us, which reduces our partner's options to indolent passivity or rebellion.

No ambiguities in either case. But also no love — and no faith.

"I no longer call you servants; I call you friends," said Jesus (John 15:15). Is it not quite obvious that this is the model by which we understand our growing intimacy with God? Not as abject, puppy-dog submission, and certainly not as manipulative priest-craft, but as willed passivity, in imitation of and matched by the willed passivity of him who "did not count equality with God a thing to be grasped but emptied himself, being born in the likeness of men" (Phil. 2:6–7).

Willfulness or Willingness?

Gerald May, in his book *Will and Spirit,* distinguishes between willfulness and willingness. Every act of intimacy, whether in work or language or marriage or prayer, suppresses willfulness and cultivates willingness.

All of us, in the act of creation, suppress willfulness and cultivate willingness. There is a deep sense of being involved in something more than the ego, better than the self. The "more" and the "better" among Christians has a personal name, *God.*

One of the qualities of will in its freedom is knowing the nature and extent of the necessities in which it works. Unmindful of necessities, the will becomes arrogant and liable to hubris (which the Greeks saw as inevitably punished with tragedy) or timidly declines to couch-potato lethargy indistinguishable from vegetation. Humble boldness (or, bold humility) enters into a sane, robust willing — free willing — and finds its most expressive and satisfying experience in prayer to Jesus Christ, who wills our salvation.

X

The Ministry of Small Talk

Blessed are the merciful

A billion years of pummeling surf,
Shipwrecking seachanges and Jonah storms
Made ungiving, unforgiving granite
Into this analgesic beach:
Washed by sea-swell rhythms of mercy,
Merciful relief from city
Concrete. Uncondemned, discalceate,
I'm ankle deep in Assateague sands,
Awake to rich designs of compassion
Patterned in the pillowing dunes.
Sandpipers and gulls in skittering,
Precise formation devoutly attend
My salt and holy solitude,
Then feed and fly along the moving,
Imprecise ebb- and rip-tide
Border dividing care from death.

My PASTOR, during my adolescent years, came often to our home. After a brief and awkward interval, he always said, "And how are things in your SOUL today?" (He always pronounced "soul" in capital letters.)

I never said much. I was too intimidated. The thoughts and experiences that filled my life in those years seemed small potatoes after that question. I knew, of course, that if I ever wanted to discuss matters of SOUL, I could go to him. But for everything else, I would probably do better with someone who wouldn't brush aside as worldly vanity what it felt like to get cut from the basketball varsity, someone who wouldn't pounce with scary intimations of hellfire on the thoughts I was having about Marnie Schmidt, the new girl from California.

Pastoral work, I learned later, is that aspect of Christian ministry that specializes in the ordinary. It is the nature of pastoral life to be attentive to, immersed in, and appreciative of the everyday texture of people's lives — the buying and selling, the visiting and meeting, the going and coming. There are also crisis events to be met: birth and death, conversion and commitment, baptism and Eucharist, despair and celebration. These also occur in people's lives and, therefore, in pastoral work. But not as everyday items.

Most people, most of the time, are not in crisis. If pastoral work is to represent the gospel and develop a life of faith in the actual circumstances of life, it must learn to be at home in what novelist William Golding has termed the "ordinary universe" — the everyday things in people's lives — getting kids off to school, deciding what to have for dinner, dealing with the daily droning complaints of work associates, watching the nightly news on TV, making small talk at coffee break.

Small talk: the way we talk when we aren't talking about anything in particular, when we don't have to think logically, or decide sensibly, or understand accurately. The reassuring conversational noises that make no demands, inflict no stress. The sounds that take the pressure off. The meandering talk that simply expresses what is going on at the time. My old pastor's refusal (or inability) to engage in that kind of talk implied, in effect, that most of my life was being lived at a subspiritual level. Vast tracts of my experience were "worldly," with occasional moments qualifying as "spiritual." I never questioned the practice until I became a pastor myself and found that such an approach left me uninvolved with most of what was happening in people's lives and without a conversational context for the actual undramatic work of living by faith in the fog and the drizzle.

Impatient with the Ordinary

Given a choice between heated discussion on theories of the Atonement and casual banter over the prospects of the coming Little League season, I didn't hesitate. It was the Atonement every time. If someone in the room raised questions of eschatology, it wasn't long before I was in the thick of the talk, but if conversation dipped to the sale on radial tires at the local dealer's, my attention flagged. I substituted meaningless nods and grunts while looking for a way to disengage myself and get on to a more urgent and demanding meeting of souls. What time did I have for small talk when I was committed to the large message of salvation and eternity? What did I have to do with the desultory gossip of weather and politics when I had "fire in my mouth"?

I know I am not the only pastor who has been ill at ease and impatient with small talk. And I know I am not the only pastor who has rationalized impatience by claiming big-talk priorities of Sermons and Apologetics and Counsel.

The rationalization seems plausible. After spending so much time learning the subtleties of supralapsarianism, surely it is wasteful to talk of the Pittsburgh Pirates. "Redeem the time!" With warehouses of knowledge stored in our brain cells, what business do we have chatting about Cabbage Patch dolls? If we have any chance at all in setting the agenda for conversation, are we not obligated to make it something spiritually important? And if we can't set the agenda, isn't it our task to work the conversation around to what our calling and training have equipped us to bring home to people's hearts?

The practice of manipulating conversation was widely used among people I respected in my college and seminary years, and I was much influenced by them. Their conviction was that every conversation could be turned, if we were sharp enough, into witness. A casual conversation on an airplane could be turned into an eternity-fraught conversation on the soul. A brief interchange with a filling-station attendant could yield the opening for a "word for Christ."

Such approaches to conversation left no room for small talk — all small talk was manipulated into big talk: of Jesus, of salvation, of the soul's condition.

Small Talk: A Pastoral Art

But however appropriate such verbal strategies are for certain instances of witness (and I think there are such instances), as habitual *pastoral* practice they are wrong. If we bully people into talking on our terms, if we manipulate them into responding to our agenda, we do not take them seriously where they are in the ordinary and the everyday.

Nor are we likely to become aware of the tiny shoots of green grace that the Lord is allowing to grow in the back yards of their lives. If we avoid small talk, we abandon the very field in which we have been assigned to work. Most of people's lives is not spent in crisis, not lived at the cutting edge of crucial issues. Most of us, most of the time, are engaged in simple, routine tasks, and small talk is the natural language. If pastors belittle it, we belittle what most people are doing most of the time, and the gospel is misrepresented.

"Lord, how I loathe big issues!" is a sentence I copied from one of C. S. Lewis's letters and have kept as a reminder. He was reacting to pretentiousness that only sees significance in the headlines — in the noisy and large. Lewis warned of the nose-in-the-air arrogance that is oblivious to the homely and the out-of-the-way, and therefore misses participating in most of the rich reality of existence.

Pastors especially, since we are frequently involved with large truths and are stewards of great mysteries, need to cultivate conversational humility. Humility means staying close to the ground (*humus*), to people, to everyday life, to what is happening with all its down-to-earthness.

I do not want to be misunderstood: pastoral conversation should not bound along on mindless clichés like gutter water. What I intend is that we simply be present and attentive to what is there conversationally, as respectful of the ordinary as we are of the critical. Some insights are only accessible while laughing. Others arrive only by indirection.

Art is involved here. Art means that we give ourselves to the encounter, to the occasion, not condescendingly and not grudgingly but creatively. We're not trying to make something happen but to be part of what is happening — without being in control of it and without it being up to the dignity of our office.

Such art develops better when we are convinced that the Holy Spirit is "beforehand" in all our meetings and conversations. I don't think it is stretching things to see Jesus — who embraced little children, which so surprised and scandalized his followers — also embracing our little conversations.

We mount our Sinai pulpits week by week and proclaim the gospel in what we hope is the persuasive authority of "artful thunder" (Emerson's phrase). When we descend to the people on the plain, a different artfulness is required, the art of small talk.

XI

Unwell in a New Way

Blessed are the pure in heart

Austere country, this, scrubbed
By spring's ravaging avalanche.
Talus slope and Appekunny
Mudstone make a meadow where
High-country beargrass gathers light
From lichen, rock, and icy tarn,
Changing sun's lethal rays
To food for grizzlies, drink for bees —
Heart-pure creatures living blessed
Under the shining of God's face.
Yet, like us the far-fallen,
Neither can they look on the face
And live. Every blossom's a breast
Holding eventual sight for all blind and
Groping newborn: we touch our way
Through these splendors to the glory.

A TUG OF WAR takes place every week between pastor and people. The contest is over conflicting views of the person who comes to church. The result of the struggle is exhibited in the service of worship, shaping sermon and prayers, influencing gesture and tone.

People (and particularly people who come to church and put themselves in touch with pastoral ministry) see themselves in human and moral terms: they have human needs that need fulfilling and moral deficiencies that need correcting. Pastors see people quite differently. We see them in theological terms: they are sinners — persons separated from God who need to be restored in Christ.

These two views — the pastor's theological understanding of people and the people's self-understanding — are almost always in tension.

Seeing People as Sinners

The word *sinner* is a theological designation. It is essential to insist on this. It is *not* a moralistic judgment. It is not a word that places humans somewhere along a continuum ranging from angel to ape, assessing them as relatively "good" or "bad." It designates humans in relation to God and sees them separated from God. *Sinner* means something is awry between humans and God. In that state people may be wicked, unhappy, anxious, and poor. Or, they may be virtuous, happy, and affluent. Those items are not part of the judgment. The theological fact is that humans are not close to God and are not serving God.

To see a person as sinner, then, is not to see him or her as hypocritical, disgusting, or evil. Most sinners are very nice people. To call a man a sinner is not a blast at his manners or his morals. It is a theological belief that the thing that matters most to him is forgiveness and grace.

If a pastor finds himself resenting his people, getting petulant and haranguing them, that is a sign that he or she has quit thinking of them as sinners who bring "nothing in themselves of worth" and has secretly invested them with divine attributes of love, strength, compassion, and joy. They, of course, do not have these attributes in any mature measure and so will disappoint him or her every time. On the other hand, if the pastor rigorously defines people as fellow sinners, he or she will be prepared to share grief, shortcomings, pain, failure, and have plenty of time left over to watch for the signs of God's grace operating in this wilderness, and then fill the air with praises for what he discovers.

An understanding of people as sinners enables a pastoral ministry to function without anger. Accumulated resentment (a constant threat to pastors) is dissolved when unreal — that is, untheological — presuppositions are abandoned. If people are sinners then pastors can concentrate on talking about God's action in Jesus Christ instead of sitting around lamenting how bad the people are. We already know they can't make it. We already have accepted their depravity. We didn't engage to be pastor to relax in their care or entrust ourselves to their saintly ways. "Cursed be he that trusteth in man, even if he be a pious man, or, perhaps, particularly if he be a pious man" (Reinhold Niebuhr). We have come among the people to talk about Jesus Christ. Grace is the main subject of pastoral conversation and preaching. "Where sin increased, grace abounded all the more" (Rom. 5:20).

But a pastor is not likely to find this view of people supported by the people themselves. They ordinarily assume that everyone has a divine inner core that needs awakening. They're Emersonian in their presuppositions, not Pauline. They expect personal help from the pastor in the shape of moralistic, mystic, or intellectual endeavors. People don't reckon with sin as that total fact that characterizes them; nor do they long for forgiveness as the effective remedy. They yearn for the nurture of their psychic life, for a way in which they may bypass grace and walk on their own. They are frequently noble and sincere in their approach as they ask the pastor to believe in them and their inner resources and possibilities. The pastor can easily be moved to accommodate such self-understanding. But it is a way without grace. The pastor must not give in. This road must be blocked. The Word of God to which pastoral ministry is committed loses propinquity the moment a person is not understood as a sinner.

The happy result of a theological understanding of people as sinners is that the pastor is saved from continual surprise that they are in fact sinners. It enables us to heed Bonhoeffer's admonition: "A pastor should not complain about his congregation, certainly never to other people, but also not to God. A congregation has not been entrusted to him in order that he should become its accuser before God and men." So *sinner* becomes not a weapon in an arsenal of condemnation, but the expectation of grace. Simply to be against sin is a poor basis for pastoral ministry. But to see people as sinners — as rebels against God, missers of the mark, wanderers from the way — *that* establishes a basis for pastoral ministry that can proceed with great joy because it is announcing God's great action in Jesus Christ "for sinners."

Discerning Sin's Particular Forms

There is more to it, though, than establishing a theological viewpoint. If the pastor first of all has to be a theologian in order to see people accurately, he or she must quickly acquire pastoral insights into the particular way sin expresses itself. Sin, for pastors, does not remain a theological rubric; it takes on specific human forms that call out specific pastoral responses. There is a great peril in conveying too abstract an idea of it. Sin is not simply a failure in relation to God that can be studied lexically; it is a personal deviation from God's will. Pastors deal with stories, not definitions, of sin. The pastor enters the world of the local and the personal. He or she seeks to establish in the language and images of everyday life the bare fact that the Christian life is possible within the chronological boundaries of a person's life and in the geographical vicinity of his or her street address.

So however necessary it is to have a theological under-standing of people as sinners, the pastor is not ready for ministry until he or she finds the particular forms that sin takes in individual histories. The pastor presses for details. He (or she) is interested in exactly *how* people are sinners. *That* they are sinners he accepts as a presupposition — he wouldn't be preaching the "foolishness of the cross" if he hadn't accepted that. But there are different ways of being a sinner. Pastoral ministry increases in effectiveness as it discerns and discriminates among the forms of sin, and then loves, prays, witnesses, converses, and preaches the details of grace appropriate to each human face that takes shape in the pew.

Episodes of Adolescence

Each generation is, in poet John Berryman's words, "unwell in a new way." The way in which the present generation is unwell — that is, the forms under which it experiences sin — is through episodes of adolescence. There was a time when ideas and living styles were initiated in the adult world and filtered down to youth. Now the movement goes the other way: life-styles are generated at the youth level and pushed upward. Dress fashions, hair styles, music, and morals that are adopted by youth are evangelically pushed on an adult world, which in turn seems eager to be converted. Youth culture began as a kind of fad and then grew into a movement. Today it is nearly fascist in its influence, forcing its perceptions and styles on everyone whether he likes it or not.

This observation helps plot a pastoral understanding of people. There is a miasmic spread of the adolescent experience upward through the generations. Instead of being over and done with when the twenty-first birthday is reached, it infects the upper generations as well. It is common to see adults in their thirties, forties, and fifties who have not only adopted the external trappings of the youth culture but are actually experiencing the emotions, traumas, and difficulties typical of youth. They are experiencing life under its adolescent forms. The sins of the sons, it seems, are being visited upon the fathers.

Reference to two adolescent characteristics will illustrate this way of understanding people in pastoral ministry.

The Sense of Inadequacy

The first is a sense of inadequacy. People don't feel they are very good at the Christian life. They are apologetic and defensive about their faith.

A feeling of inadequacy is characteristic of adolescent life. When a person is growing rapidly on all fronts — physical, emotional, mental — he or she is left without competence in anything. Life doesn't slow down long enough for him to gain a sense of mastery. The teenager has a variety of devices to disguise this feeling: he can mask it with braggadocio, submerge it in a crowd of peers, or develop a subcult of language and dress in which he maintains superiority by excluding the larger world from his special competence. The variations are endless; the situation is the same: the adolescent is immature, and therefore inadequate. And he is acutely self-conscious about this inadequacy.

This is exactly what the pastor meets in people of all ages in the church. They feel they aren't making it as Christians. This is a bit of surprise because in the past the Christian church has more often had to deal with the Pharisee — the person who feels he achieved adequacy long ago. People today are much more apt to be uneasy and fearful about their Christian identity.

The ostensible reason is that the new world is changing so fast that no one gets a chance to feel at home in it. The adult, like the adolescent, is confronted with a new world every week or so and doesn't feel that he or she can cope. When this adult enters the church, he or she looks at the pastor and supposes that the *minister,* at least, has feet on the ground and knows where things are. People look at the pastor as the person with competence in things that have to do with God and cast him or her in the role of expert. That process seems natural and innocent — as natural and innocent as the feelings of inadequacy in the adolescent and his consequent admiration of competence. It is more likely, though, a new disguise for an old sin — the ancient business of making idols. God calls people to himself, but they turn away to something less than God, fashioning a religious experience but avoiding God. The excuse is that they are "inadequate" for facing the real thing. They proceed with the awareness that, far from sinning, they have acquired the virtue of humility. But the theological nose smells idolatry.

Some pastors take deliberate steps to counteract their image as substitute God by sprinkling profanity through their syntax and quoting *Playboy* magazine. They say, in effect, to the people, "I am no more adequate than you are. Don't look to me as any kind of saint; don't model your life on what I am doing." But pastoral ministry must consist of something other than disclaimers.

There is a Pauline technique for dealing with this sense of inadequacy. Writing to the Ephesians, Paul says: "For this reason, because I have heard of your faith in the Lord Jesus and your love toward all the saints, I do not cease to give thanks for you, remembering you in my prayers" (Eph. 1:15–16). Assuming that the Ephesian church had the same percentage of sinners in it as modern ones do (namely, 100 percent), it would be a mistake to envy Paul his congregation, a congregation that it was possible to address so gratefully. It is better to admire Paul's ability to see God's action in those people. Paul had a meticulous eye for the signs of grace. He was God's spy, searching out the congregational terrain for evidence that the Holy Spirit had been there. Paul knew the people were sinners. But his passion was for describing grace and opening their eyes to what his eyes were open to — the activity of God in their lives, "his power in us who believe" (Eph. 1:19).

If the pastor sees inadequacy as an unfortunate feeling, he or she will use psychological and moral means to remove it. If he sees it as a sign of sin — an avoidance of personal responsibility in the awesome task of facing God in Christ — he will respond by kindly and gently presenting the living God, pointing out the ways in which God is alive in the community. The instances of courage and grace that occur every week in any congregation are staggering. Pastoral discernment that sees grace operating in a person keeps that person in touch with the living God.

Historical Amnesia

Another characteristic of the adolescent that has spread into the larger population is the absence of historical sense. The adolescent, of course, has no history. He or she has a childhood, but no accumulation of experience that transcends personal details and produces a sense of history. His world is highly personal and extremely empirical.

As a consequence, the teenager is incredibly gullible. We suppose that a person educated in fine schools by well-trained teachers would not be in any danger of superstition. We further suppose that the fact-demanding, scientific-oriented education that prevails in our schools would have sharpened the minds of the young to be perceptive in matters of evidence and logic. It doesn't happen. The reason it doesn't happen is that they have no feeling for the past, for precedents and traditions, and so have no perspective in making judgments or discerning values. They may know the facts of history and read historical novels by the dozen, but they don't feel history in their bones. It is not *their* history. The result is that they begin every problem from scratch. There is no feeling of being part of a living tradition that already has some answers worked out and some procedures worth repeating.

This state of mind, typical in adolescence, is, within certain parameters, accepted. The odd thing today is that there is no change when a person reaches adult years. The way this ahistorical anemia has become an adult trait was evident in the first landing on the moon. Everyone was caught up in a rush of historical speculation, including President Nixon himself, who rather recklessly declared it to be the most important day in human history, thereby scandalizing his spiritual director Billy Graham by forgetting so easily the birth of Christ. When these same people come to church, the pastor discovers that they have little consciousness of being part of a community that carries in its Scriptures, its worship, and its forms of obedience a life twenty and more centuries in the making.

Such people are subject to consistent trivialization. They find it impossible to tell what may be important. They buy things, both material and spiritual, that they will never use. They hear the same lies over and over again without ever becoming angry. They are led to entertain, and for brief times practice, all kinds of religious commitment from magazine moralisms to occultic séances. In none of it do they show any particular perseverance. But neither do they show much sign of wising up — of developing a historical sense, of becoming conscious that they are part of a continuing people of God and growing beyond the adolescent susceptibilities to novelty and fantasy.

If the pastor interprets this as a form of cultural deprivation, he or she will become a pedagogue, trying to teach the people who they are as Christians, extending their memory backward. But that would be a mistake, for it is not basically a cultural condition. What begins as a normal characteristic of adolescence, when stretched into Christian adulthood, becomes a clever ruse (largely unconscious) for masking sin: the sin is a denial of dependence on God and interdependence among neighbors, a refusal to be a *people* of God and a counter-insistence that the individual ego be treated as something god-like. In the Garden of Eden the decision to substitute firsthand experience for obedience to the command of God produced in a single generation a murder that revealed its loss of history and community in the flip but exceedingly lonely question, "Am I my brother's keeper?"

Ezekiel was pastor to a similarly constituted people, who by refusing to be responsible to God and each other had lost a sense of history. His ministry provides insight into a style of pastoral response. Israel was severed from its roots, the old rituals and traditions didn't appear to have relevance in the land of exile, and people were easy prey to their heathen environment. Everyone was subject to the temptation to try to make it on his or her own, fashioning a religion out of personal basic survival needs. In this time of need, what Ezekiel did *not* do was start a school and teach history lessons. Rather he preached a new life, exposed the nature of the people's sin, and appealed to their conscience to be made into a new people by God's grace. A foundation was established in the covenant life of the people of God that, in contrast to the cultural and economic conceptions of the ancient East (and modern West!), protected the divine value of every person, showing a way of salvation and promising a future. People were asked to let themselves be taken into personal relationships of service and loyalty to the God who releases them from the chain of guilt down the generations and gives them a new start by forgiving them and then guaranteeing them a life and a future. They were reinserted into a community with a history.

Undoubtedly this development first took place in the prophet's own house where the elders (Ezek. 8:1; 12:9; 14:1; 20:1; 24:19) and other members of the colony in Babylon (33:30–33) gathered in order to hear some word from God or obtain advice about various problems. Many were superficial and came merely out of curiosity, but that did not prevent the prophet from finding some who responded to his appeal for a decision to repent and be made new by God. As a result, in meetings that had previously been held in order to keep up and preserve ancient, inherited spiritual possessions, hopelessly trying to defend against the loss of history that the exile produced, the Holy Spirit brought new expectations and resolutions to life. A new community was established with a lively sense of the past recast in bright visions of the future (chaps.

40–48). Ezekiel saw that the problem among the people was not historical ignorance, although they were ignorant that way. Perceptively, he diagnosed the sin that was using "loss of history" as a front, and convincingly preached a word of grace.

The Quick Theological Eye

The people encountered in pastoral ministry today are sinners. But they don't look like it, and many of them don't even act like it. They rather look and act and feel like the youth they admire so much, struggling for "identity" and searching for "integrity." A quick theological eye that is able to pick up the movements of sin hiding behind these seemingly innocent characteristics will keep a pastor on track, doing what he or she was called to do: sharing a ministry of grace and forgiveness centered in Jesus Christ.

XII

Lashed to the Mast

Blessed are the peacemakers

Huge cloud fists assault
The blue exposed bare midriff of sky:
The firmament doubles up in pain.
Lightnings rip and thunders shout;
Mother nature's children quarrel.
And then, as suddenly as it began,
It's over. Noah's heirs, perceptions
Cleansed, look out on a disarmed world
At ease and ozone fragrant. Still waters.
What barometric shift
Rearranged these ferocities
Into a peace-pulsating rainbow
Sign? My enemy turns his other
Cheek; I drop my guard. A mirror
Lake reflects the filtered colors;
Breeze-stirred pine trees quietly sing.

Anne Tyler, in her novel *Morgan's Passing*, told the story of a middle-aged Baltimore man who passed through people's lives with astonishing aplomb and expertise in assuming roles and gratifying expectations.

The novel opens with Morgan's watching a puppet show on a church lawn on a Sunday afternoon. A few minutes into the show, a young man comes from behind the puppet stage and asks, "Is there a doctor here?" After thirty or forty seconds with no response from the audience, Morgan stands up, slowly and deliberately approaches the young man, and asks, "What is the trouble?" The puppeteer's pregnant wife is in labor; a birth seems imminent. Morgan puts the young couple in the back of his station wagon and sets off for Johns Hopkins Hospital. Halfway there the husband says, "The baby is coming!"

Morgan, calm and self-assured, pulls to the curb, sends the about-to-be father to the corner to buy a Sunday paper as a substitute for towels and bed sheets, and delivers the baby. He then drives to the emergency room of the hospital, sees the mother and baby safely to a stretcher, and disappears. After the excitement dies down, the couple asks for Dr. Morgan to thank him. But no one has ever heard of a Dr. Morgan. They are puzzled — and frustrated that they can't express their gratitude.

Several months later they are pushing their baby in a stroller and see Morgan walking on the other side of the street. They run over and greet him, showing him the healthy baby that he brought into the world. They tell him how hard they had looked for him, and of the hospital's bureaucratic incompetence in tracking him down. In an unaccustomed gush of honesty, he admits to them that he is not really a doctor. In fact, he runs a hardware store. But they needed a doctor, and being a doctor in those circumstances was not all that difficult.

It is an image thing, he tells them: You discern what people expect and fit into it. You can get by with it in all the honored professions. He has been doing this all his life, impersonating doctors, lawyers, pastors, counselors as occasions present themselves.

Then he confides, "You know, I would never pretend to be a plumber or impersonate a butcher — they would find me out in twenty seconds."

Morgan knew something that most pastors catch on to early in their work: the image aspects of pastoring, the parts that require meeting people's expectations, can be faked. We can impersonate a pastor without being a pastor. The problem, though, is that while we can get by with it in our communities, often with applause, we can't get by with it within ourselves.

At least, not all of us can. Some of us get restive. We feel awful. No level of success seems to be insurance against an eruption of *angst* in the middle of our applauded performance.

The restiveness does not come from puritanical guilt; we *are* doing what we're paid to do. The people who pay our salaries are getting their money's worth. We are "giving good weight" — the sermons are inspiring, the committees are efficient, the morale is good. The restiveness comes from another dimension — from a vocational memory, a spiritual hunger, a professional commitment.

The Danger of Doing the Job

Being a pastor who satisfies a congregation is one of the easiest jobs on the face of the earth — *if* we are satisfied with satisfying congregations. The hours are good, the pay is adequate, the prestige considerable. Why don't we find it easy? Why aren't we content with it?

Because we set out to do something quite different. We set out to risk our lives in a venture of faith. We committed ourselves to a life of holiness. At some point we realized the immensity of God and of the great invisibles that socket into our arms and legs, into bread and wine, into our brains and our tools, into mountains and rivers, giving them meaning, destiny, value, joy, beauty, salvation. We responded to a call to convey these realities in Word and sacrament. We offered ourselves to give leadership that connects and coordinates what the people in this community of faith are doing in their work and play, with what God is doing in mercy and grace.

In the process, we learned the difference between a profession, a craft, and a job.

A job is what we do to complete an assignment. Its primary requirement is that we give satisfaction to whoever makes the assignment and pays our wage. We learn what is expected and we do it. There is nothing wrong with doing jobs. To a lesser or greater extent, we all have them; somebody has to wash the dishes and take out the garbage.

But professions and crafts are different. In these we have an obligation beyond pleasing somebody; we are pursuing or shaping the very nature of reality, convinced that when we carry out our commitments, we benefit people at a far deeper level than if we simply did what they asked of us.

In crafts we are dealing with visible realities, in professions with invisible. The craft of woodworking, for instance, has an obligation to the wood itself, its grain and texture. A good woodworker knows his woods and treats them with respect. Far more is involved than pleasing customers; something like integrity of material is involved.

With professions the integrity has to do with the invisibles: for physicians it is health (not merely making people feel good); with lawyers, justice (not helping people get their own way);

with professors, learning (not cramming cranial cavities with information on tap for examinations). And with pastors, it is God (not relieving anxiety, or giving comfort, or running a religious establishment).

We all start out knowing this, or at least having a pretty good intimation of it. But when we entered our first parish, we were given a job.

Most of the people we deal with are dominated by a sense of self, not a sense of God. Insofar as we deal with their primary concern — the counseling, instructing, encouraging — they give us good marks in our *jobs* as pastors. Whether we deal with God or not, they don't care over much. Flannery O'Connor describes one pastor in such circumstances as one part minister and three parts masseur.

It is very difficult to do one thing when most of the people around us are asking us to do something quite different, especially when these people are nice, intelligent, treat us with respect, and pay our salaries. We get up each morning and the telephone rings, people meet us, letters are addressed to us — often at a tempo of bewildering urgency. All these calls and letters are from people who are asking us to do something for them, quite apart from any belief in God. That is, they come to us not because they are looking for God but because they are looking for a recommendation, or good advice, or an opportunity, and they vaguely suppose we might be qualified to give it to them.

A number of years ago, I injured my knee. According to my self-diagnosis, I knew all it needed was some whirlpool treatments. In my college years we had a whirlpool in the training room, and I had considerable experience with its effectiveness in treating my running injuries as well as making me feel good. In my present community, the only whirlpool was at the physical therapist's office. I called to make an appointment. He refused; I had to have a doctor's prescription.

I called an orthopedic physician, went in for an examination (this was getting more complicated and expensive than I had planned), and found he wouldn't give me the prescription for the whirlpool. He said it wasn't the proper treatment for my injury. He recommended surgery. I protested: a whirlpool certainly can't do any harm, and it might do some good. His refusal was adamantine. He was a professional. His primary commitment was to some invisible abstraction called health, healing. He was not committed to satisfying my requests. His integrity, in fact, forbade him to satisfy my requests if they encroached on his primary commitment.

I have since learned that with a little shopping around, I could have found a doctor who would have given me the prescription I wanted.

I reflect on that incident occasionally. Am I keeping the line clear between what I am committed to and what people are asking of me? Is my primary orientation God's grace, his mercy, his action in Creation and covenant? And am I committed to it enough that when people ask me to do something that will not lead them into a more mature participation in these realities, I refuse? I don't like to think of all my visits made, counseling given, marriages performed, meetings attended, prayers offered — one friend calls it sprinkling holy water on Cabbage Patch dolls — solely because people asked me to do it and it didn't seem at the time that it would do any harm and, who knows, it might do some good. Besides, I knew there was a pastor down the street who would do anything asked of him. But his theology was so wretched he would probably do active harm in the process. My theology, at least, was orthodox.

How do I keep the line sharp? How do I maintain a sense

of pastoral vocation in a community of people who hire me to do religious jobs? How do I keep professional integrity in the midst of a people long practiced in comparative shopping, who don't get overly exercised on the fine points of pastoral integrity?

Entering the Wreckage

An illusion-bashing orientation helps. Take a long look at the sheer quantity of wreckage around us — wrecked bodies, wrecked marriages, wrecked careers, wrecked plans, wrecked families, wrecked alliances, wrecked friendships, wrecked prosperity. We avert our eyes. We try not to dwell on it. We whistle in the dark. We wake up in the morning hoping for health and love, justice and success; build quick mental and emotional defenses against the inrush of bad news; and try to keep our hopes up.

And then another kind of crash puts us or someone we care about in a pile of wreckage. Newspapers document the ruins with photographs and headlines. Our own hearts and journals fill in the details. Are there any promises, any hopes exempt from the general carnage? It doesn't seem so.

Pastors walk into these ruins every day. Why do we do it? What do we hope to accomplish? After all these centuries, things don't seem to have gotten much better; do we think another day's effort is going to stay the avalanche to doomsday? Why do we not all become cynics? Is it sheer naiveté that keeps some pastors investing themselves in acts of compassion, inviting people to a life of sacrifice, suffering abuse in order to witness to the truth, stubbornly repeating an old, hard-to-believe, and much-denied story of good news in the midst of bad news?

Is our talk of citizenship in a kingdom of God anything

that can be construed as the "real world"? Or are we passing on a spiritual fiction analogous to the science fictions that fantasize a better world than we will ever live in? Is pastoral work mostly a matter of putting plastic flowers in people's drab lives — well-intentioned attempts to brighten a bad scene, not totally without use, but not real in any substantive or living sense?

Many people think so, and most pastors have moments when they think so. If we think so often enough, we slowly but inexorably begin to adopt the majority opinion and shape our work to the expectations of a people for whom God is not so much a person as a legend, who suppose that the kingdom will be wonderful once we get past Armageddon, but we had best work right now on the terms that *this* world gives us, and who think that the Good News is nice — the way greeting card verse is nice — but in no way necessary to everyday life in the way that a computer manual or a job description is.

Two facts: the general environment of wreckage provides daily and powerful stimuli to make us want to repair and fix what is wrong; the secular mindset, in which God/king-dom/gospel are not counted as primary, living realities, is constantly seeping into our imaginations. The combination — ruined world, secular mind — makes for a steady, unrelenting pressure to readjust our conviction of what pastoral work is. We're tempted to respond to the appalling conditions around us in terms that make sense to those who are appalled.

Ministering as People Set Apart

The definition that pastors start out with, given to us in our ordination, is that pastoral work is a ministry of Word and sacrament.

Word. But in the wreckage, all words sound like "mere words."

Sacrament. But in the wreckage, what difference can water, a piece of bread, a sip of wine make?

Yet century after century, Christians continue to take certain persons in their communities, set them apart, and say, "You are our shepherd. Lead us to Christlikeness."

Yes, their actions will often speak different expectations, but in the deeper regions of the soul, the unspoken desire is for more than someone doing a religious job. If the unspoken were uttered, it would sound like this:

"We want you to be responsible for saying and acting among us what we believe about God and kingdom and gospel. We believe that the Holy Spirit is among us and within us. We believe that God's Spirit continues to hover over the chaos of the world's evil and our sin, shaping a new creation and new creatures. We believe that God is not a spectator, in turn amused and alarmed at the wreckage of world history, but a participant.

"We believe that the invisible is more important than the visible at any one single moment and in any single event that we choose to examine. We believe that everything, especially everything that looks like wreckage, is material God is using to make a praising life.

"We *believe* all this, but we don't *see* it. We see, like Ezekiel, dismembered skeletons whitened under a pitiless Babylonian sun. We see a lot of bones that once were laughing and dancing children, adults who once aired their doubts and sang their praises in church — and sinned. We don't see the dancers or the lovers or the singers — or at best catch only fleeting glimpses of them. What we see are bones. Dry bones. We see sin and judgment on the sin. That is what it *looks* like. It looked that way to Ezekiel; it looks that way to anyone with eyes to see and brain to think; and it looks that way to us.

"But we *believe* something else. We believe in the coming together of these bones into connected, sinewed, muscled human beings who speak and sing and laugh and work and believe and bless their God. We believe it happened the way Ezekiel preached it, and we believe it still happens. We believe it happened in Israel and that it happens in church. We believe we are a part of the happening as we sing our praises, listen believingly to God's Word, receive the new life of Christ in the sacraments. We believe the most significant thing that happens or can happen is that we are no longer dismembered but are remembered into the resurrection body of Christ.

"We need help in keeping our beliefs sharp and accurate and intact. We don't trust ourselves; our emotions seduce us into infidelities. We know we are launched on a difficult and dangerous act of faith, and there are strong influences intent on diluting or destroying it. We want you to give us help. Be our pastor, a minister of Word and sacrament in the middle of this world's life. Minister with Word and sacrament in all the different parts and stages of our lives — in our work and play, with our children and our parents, at birth and death, in our celebrations and sorrows, on those days when morning breaks over us in a wash of sunshine, and those other days that are all drizzle. This isn't the only task in the life of faith, but it is your task. We will find someone else to do the other important and essential tasks. This is *yours*: Word and sacrament.

"One more thing: We are going to ordain you to this ministry, and we want your vow that you will stick to it. This is not a temporary job assignment but a way of life that we need lived out in our community. We know you are launched on the same difficult belief venture in the same dangerous world as we are. We know your emotions are as fickle as ours, and your mind is as tricky as ours. That is why we are going to *ordain* you and why we are going to exact a *vow* from you. We know there will be days and months, maybe even years, when we won't feel like believing anything and won't want to hear it from you. And we know there will be days and weeks and maybe even years when you won't feel like saying it. It doesn't matter. Do it. You are ordained to this ministry, vowed to it.

"There may be times when we come to you as a committee or delegation and demand that you tell us something else than what we are telling you now. Promise right now that you won't give in to what we demand of you. You are not the minister of our changing desires, or our time-conditioned understanding of our needs, or our secularized hopes for something better. With these vows of ordination we are lashing you fast to the mast of Word and sacrament so you will be unable to respond to the siren voices.

"There are many other things to be done in this wrecked world, and we are going to be doing at least some of them, but if we don't know the foundational realities with which we are dealing — God, kingdom, gospel — we are going to end up living futile, fantasy lives. Your task is to keep telling the basic story, representing the presence of the Spirit, insisting on the priority of God, speaking the biblical words of command and promise and invitation."

That, or something very much like that, is what I understand the church to say — even when the people cannot articulate it — to the individuals it ordains to be its pastors.

XIII

Desert and Harvest: A Sabbatical Story

Blessed are those who are persecuted

Unfriendly waters do a friendly
Thing: curses, cataract-hurled
Stones, make the rough places
Smooth; a rushing whitewater stream
Of blasphemies hate-launched,
Then caught by the sun, sprays rainbow
Arcs across the Youghiogeny.
Savaged by the river's impersonal
Attack the land is deepened to bedrock.
Wise passivities are earned
In quiet, craggy, occasional pools
That chasten the wild waters to stillness,
And hold them under hemlock green
For birds and deer to bathe and drink
In peace — persecution's gift:
The hard-won, blessed letting be.

WE WERE both apprehensive, my wife and I. We had been away from our congregation for twelve months, a sabbatical year, and we were on our way back. It had been a wonderful year, soaking in the silence, gulping down great drafts of high-country air. Could we handle the transition from the solitude of the Montana Rockies to the traffic of Maryland?

Being a pastor is a difficult job, maybe no harder than any other job — any job done well requires everything that is in us — but hard all the same. For a year we had not done it: no interruptive phone calls, no exhilarating/exhausting creativity at pulpit and lectern, no doggedly carried out duties. We played and we prayed. We split wood and shoveled snow. We read and talked over what we read. We cross-country skied in the winter and hiked in the summer.

Every Sunday we did what we had not done for thirty years: we sat together and worshiped God. We went to the Eidsvold Lutheran Church in Somers with seventy or eighty other Christians, mostly Norwegians, and sang hymns that we didn't know very well. Pastor Pris led us in prayer and preached rich sermons.

Comfortable in the pew on an April Sunday, I had an inkling of what the pastor had been doing that week — the meetings he had attended and the crises he had endured. While the Spirit was using his sermon to speak quite personally to me, at the edges of my mind I was admiringly aware of the sheer craft, exegetically and homiletically, behind it. Then, as people who sit in church pews often do, I mentally wandered. *How does he do that week after week? How does he stay so fresh, so alert, so on target, so alive to people and Christ? And in the midst of all this stress and emotion and study and ecclesiastical shopkeeping? That's got to be the toughest job on earth — I could never do that. I'm glad I don't have a job like that.*

And then I realized, *But I do have a job like that; that is my job — or will be, again, in a few months.*

Those "few months" were now whittled down to "next week." We weren't sure we were up to it. Maybe the sabbatical, instead of refreshing us, had only spoiled us. Instead of energizing, maybe it had enervated us. For thirty years we had lived a hundred or so feet down in the ocean of parish life (how much pressure per square inch is that?) and for a year of sabbatical we had surfaced, basking in the sun, romping in the snow. Deep-sea divers enter decompression chambers as they leave the depths, lest they get the bends. We felt an equivalent need for a "recompression chamber" as we returned to the depths.

From Montana to the East Coast, Interstate 90 stretches out an inviting beeline, nearly straight, with a couple of sweeping curves (but bees also buzz curves). But we veered off on a detour south to the high desert of Colorado for a four-day retreat at a monastery. The monastery, we hoped, would be our recompression chamber. It was not as if we hadn't had time for prayer. We had never had so much time for it. But we sensed the need for something else now — a community of prayer, some friends with a vocation for prayer among whom we could immerse our vocation as pastor.

So for four days we prayed in a community that prayed. The days had an easy rhythm: morning prayers in the chapel with the monks and other retreatants at 6 o'clock; evening prayers at 5 o'clock; before and after and in between, silence — walking, reading, praying, emptying. The rhythm broke on Sunday. After morning prayers and the Eucharist, everyone met for a noisy and festive breakfast. The silence had dug wells of joy that now spilled into the community in artesian conversation and laughter.

When we left the monastery, the Montana sabbatical year

was, as we had intended in our praying, behind us emotionally as well as geographically. Three days later we arrived in Maryland, focused and explosive with energy.

Stimulus for Sabbatical

The idea for a sabbatical developed from a two-pronged stimulus: fatigue and frustration. I was tired. That's hardly unusual in itself, but it was a tiredness that vacations weren't fixing — a tiredness of spirit, an inner boredom. I sensed a spiritual core to my fatigue and was looking for a spiritual remedy.

Along the way as a pastor, I had also become a writer. I longed for a stretch of time to express some thoughts about my pastoral vocation, time that was never available while I was in the act of being a pastor.

A sabbatical year seemed to serve both needs perfectly. But how would I get it? I serve a single-pastor church, and there was no money to fund a sabbatical: Who would replace me while I was away? How would I pay for the venture? The two difficulties seemed formidable. But I felt that if the sabbatical was in fact the spiritual remedy to a spiritual need, the church ought to be able to come up with a solution.

I started by calling several of the leaders in the congregation and inviting them to my home for an evening. I told them what I felt and what I wanted. I didn't ask them to solve the problem, but asked them to enter into seeking a solution with me. They asked a lot of questions; they took me seriously; they perceived it as a congregational task; they started to see themselves as pastor to me. When the evening ended, we had not solved the difficulties, but I knew I had allies praying, working, and thinking with me. The concept of "sabbatical" filled out and developed momentum. Over a period of several months, the "mountains" moved.

Replacement: This turned out to be not much of a difficulty at all. My denomination offered help in locating an interim pastor — there are quite a few men and women who are available for just such work. We decided finally to call a young man who had recently served as an intern for a year with us.

Funding: We worked out a plan in which the church paid me one-third of my salary, and I arranged for the other two-thirds. I did this by renting out my house for the year and asking a generous friend for assistance. We had a family home on a lake in Montana where my parents, now deceased, had lived and we had always vacationed. It was suited to our needs for solitude, and we could live there inexpensively.

Detail after detail fell into place, not always easily or quickly, but after ten months the sabbatical year was agreed upon and planned. I interpreted what we were doing in a letter to the congregation:

"Sabbatical years are the biblically based provision for restoration. When the farmer's field is depleted, it is given a sabbatical — after six years of planting and harvesting, it is left alone for a year so that the nutrients can build up in it. When people in ministry are depleted, they also are given a sabbatical — time apart for the recovery of spiritual and creative energies. I have been feeling the need for just such a time of restoration for about two years. The sense that my reserves are low, that my margins of creativity are crowded, becomes more acute each week. I feel the need for some 'desert' time — for silence, for solitude, for prayer.

"One of the things I fear most as your pastor is that out of fatigue or sloth I end up going through the motions, substituting professional smoothness for personal grappling with the life of the Spirit in our life together. The demands of pastoral life are strenuous, and there is no respite from them. There are not many hours in any day when I am not faced with the struggle of faith in someone or another, the deep, central, eternal energies that make the difference between a life lived to the glory of God and a life wasted in self-indulgence or trivialized in diversions. I want to be ready for those encounters. For me, that is what it means to be a pastor: to be in touch with the Lord's Word and presence, and to be ready to speak and act out of that Word and presence in whatever I am doing — while leading you in worship, teaching Scripture, talking and praying with you individually, meeting with you in groups as we order our common life, writing poems and articles and books.

"It is in this capacity for intensity and intimacy, staying at the center where God's Word makes things alive, that I feel in need of repletion. The demands are so much greater today than they were in earlier years. One of the things that twenty-three years of pastoral life among you means is that there is a complex network of people both within and without the congregation with whom I am in significant relationship. I would not have it otherwise. But I must also do something to maintain the central springs of compassion and creativity lest it all be flattened out into routines.

"Parallel with this felt need for 'desert' time, I feel the need for 'harvest' time. These twenty-three years with you have been full and rich. I came here inexperienced and untutored. Together, taught by the Spirit and by each other, we have learned much: You have become a congregation; I have become a pastor. During this time, I realized that writing is an essential element in my pastoral vocation with you. All the writing comes out of the soil of this community of faith as we worship together, attend to Scripture, seek to discern the Spirit's presence in our lives. As I write, a growing readership expresses appreciation and affirms me in the work. Right now, so much that is mature and ripe for harvest remains unwritten. I want to write what we have lived together. I don't want to write on the run, hastily, or carelessly. I want to write this well, to the glory of God.

"Jan and I talked about this, prayed together, and consulted with persons whom we hold to be wise. The obvious solution was to accept a call to another congregation. That would provide the clean simplicity of new relationships uncomplicated by history and the stimulus of new beginnings. But we didn't want to leave here if we could find another way; the life of worship and love that we have developed together is a great treasure that we will part with only if required. We arrived at the idea of the sabbatical, a year away for prayer and writing so that we would be able to return to this place and this people and do our very best in ministry with you.

"So, a desert time and a harvest time, time for prayer and time for writing, the two times side by side, contrasting, converging, cross-fertilizing. Many of you have already given your blessing and encouragement in this venture, affirming our resolve in taking this faith-step, being obedient to God in our lives."

Structure for the Sabbatical

And so it happened. Twelve months away from my congregation. Twelve months to pray and write, to worship and walk, to converse and read, to remember and revision.

From the outset we had conceived of the sabbatical as a joint enterprise, meeting a spiritual need in both pastor and congregation. We didn't want the year to be misinterpreted as an escape; we didn't want to be viewed as "off doing their own thing." We were committed to this congregation. The sabbatical was provided to deepen and continue our common ministry. How could we convey that? How could we cultivate our intimacy in the faith and not have the geographic separation separate us spiritually?

We decided to write a monthly "Sabbatical Letter" in two parts, "Jan's side" and "Eugene's side." We sent a roll of film along with the letter; a friend developed the pictures of our life that month and displayed them in the narthex. The letters and pictures did exactly what we had hoped. But only one side of the letters seems to have been read closely — Jan's. I couldn't quit preaching. She conveyed the sabbatical experience.

Brita Stendahl wrote once that the sabbatical year she and her husband, Krister, had in Sweden "gave us our lives back." Jan's side of the sabbatical letters revealed that dimension of our year for our worshiping and believing friends at home. She set the tone in the first letter:

"Separated from us by 2,500 miles, my mother-in-law was always pleased to get a letter from us. Because Eugene was her eldest and out 'seeking adventures' both physically and ideologically, she was always glad to be stretched by his cosmic and theological letters. He would share with her all the *Big Ideas*. But being a mother and homemaker, she especially liked to hear from me because I would tell her what we were having for dinner, the latest troubles or triumphs of her grandchildren, the rips in their clothing, and the precocious oracles from their mouths. You can read the *Big Ideas* on the other side of the page, but here is my mother-in-law letter to you, our dear family at Christ Our King.

"The trip across the country was good. We camped out a couple of nights on the way. We took to heart most of the well-wishing advice you gave us as we left, but the numerous admonitions to dress warmly didn't 'take.' Our first night in

Montana we camped at the headwaters of the Missouri River and managed to freeze the particular extremity that it isn't proper to mention in a church newsletter. We brought the dog into the tent for added warmth, but she wasn't as much help as we needed. The night sky was stunning with its brilliant stars all the way down to the horizon. (I never knew stars went all the way down to the horizon!) The tent was ice coated in the morning.

"The first week here has been spent cleaning, rearranging, and trying to get the house warm enough. I think I am finally getting the knack of building a wood fire. We have interspersed our settling in with walks in the woods and reading aloud to each other (Garrison Keillor right now).

"One day we took off for Glacier Park to see dozens of bald eagles fishing for the salmon spawning in MacDonald Creek. Last year on the peak day, over five hundred were sighted. After our birding we hiked to Avalanche Lake, two and one-half miles up into a glacial cirque. It was a day marvelous in weather — snow flurries, sun, wind, clouds.

"We have about thirty ducks swimming around our bay here on the lake. Last Sunday we returned from worship and saw a furry creature on our dock licking himself dry and realized it was a mink.

"Eric and Lynn came over from Spokane for the weekend. We had Eugene's brother and sister and their families for a potluck Friday evening. That was a happy reunion and a good time. One of our prayers for this year is that our family gatherings will be rich and full.

"One of the last things that we asked Mabel Scarborough to do for us before leaving Bel Air was to update a church directory so that we could pray for you, our faith family, each day. Be assured of our love and our prayers. We feel very close to you. For supper tonight we had creamed tuna over sourdough biscuits."

Such was the nature of our time. Once we arrived in Montana, we established a routine to support our twin goals of desert and harvest so that we would not fritter away the year. We agreed on a five-day work week, with Saturday and Sunday given to playing and praying. I worked hard for about five hours a day at my writing desk and then relaxed. We had evening prayers in the late afternoon and followed that by reading aloud to each other and fixing supper. After nine months of this, I had the two books written that I had set out to complete (the "harvest"). From then on it was all "desert" — reading and praying and hiking.

Refit for Ministry

Everything I had hoped for came to pass: I returned with more energy than I can remember having since I was fifteen years old. I have always (with occasional, but brief, lapses) enjoyed being a pastor. But never this much. The experience of my maturity was now coupled with the energy of my youth, a combination I had not thought possible. The parts of pastoral work I had done out of duty before, just because somebody had to do them, I now embraced with delight. I felt deep reservoirs within me, capacious and free flowing. I felt great margins of leisure around everything I did — conversations, meetings, letter writing, telephone calls. I felt I would never again be in a hurry. The sabbatical had done its work.

A benefit I had not counted on was a change in the congregation. They were refreshed and confident in a way I had not observed before. One of the dangers of a long-term pastorate is the development of neurotic dependencies between pastor and people. I had worried about that from time to time:

Was it healthy of me to stay in this congregation for so long? Had I taken the place of God for them?

Those fears became more acute when I proposed the sabbatical year, for many people expressed excessive anxiety — anxiety that I would not return, anxiety that the church could not get along without me, anxiety that the life of faith and worship and trust that we had worked so hard to develop would disintegrate in my absence. None of these fears was realized. Not one. Not even a little bit. The congregation thrived. They found they did not need me at all. They discovered they could be a church of Jesus Christ with another pastor quite as well as they could with me. I returned to a congregation confident in its maturity as a people of God.

A recent incident, seemingly trivial, illustrates the profound difference that keeps showing up in a variety of situations. About twenty-five of us were going on an overnight leadership retreat. We had agreed to meet in the church parking lot at 5:45 to car-pool together. I made a hospital visit that took longer than planned and arrived five minutes late — to an empty parking lot. They had left me. Before the sabbatical, that would never have happened; now that kind of thing happens all the time. They can take care of themselves and know that I can take care of myself. Maturity.

We are both, the congregation and I, experiencing a great freedom in this: neither of us neurotically *needs* each other. I am not dependent on them; they aren't dependent on me. That leaves us free to appreciate each other and receive gifts of ministry from each other.

THE WORD
MADE FRESH

XIV

Poets and Pastors

Is it not significant that the biblical prophets and psalmists were all poets?

Pastors and poets do many things in common: use words with reverence, get immersed in everyday particulars, spy out the glories of the commonplace, warn of illusions, attend to the subtle interconnections between rhythm and meaning and spirit. I think we ought to seek each other out as friends and allies.

Poets are caretakers of language, the shepherds of words, keeping them from harm, exploitation, misuse. Words not only mean something; they are something, each with a sound and rhythm all its own.

Poets are not primarily trying to tell us, or get us, to do something. By attending to words with playful discipline (or disciplined playfulness), they draw us into deeper respect both for words and for the reality they set before us.

Pastors are also in the word business. We preach, teach, and counsel using words. People often pay particular attention on the chance that God may be using our words to speak to them. We have a responsibility to use words accurately and well. But it isn't easy. We live in a world where words are used carelessly by some, cunningly by others.

It is so easy for us to say whatever comes to mind, our role as pastor compensating for our inane speech. It is easy to say what either flatters or manipulates and so acquire power over others. In subtle ways, being a pastor subjects our words to corruption. That is why it is important to frequent the company of a poet friend — Gerard Manley Hopkins, George Herbert, Emily Dickinson, Luci Shaw are some of mine — a person who cares about words and is honest with them, who respects and honors their sheer overwhelming power. I leave such meetings less careless, my reverence for words and the Word restored.

Is it not significant that the biblical prophets and psalmists were all poets? It is a continuing curiosity that so many pastors, whose work integrates the prophetic and psalmic (preaching and praying), are indifferent to poets. In reading poets, I find congenial allies in the world of words. In writing poems, I find myself practicing my pastoral craft in a biblical way.

The following poems work off of the pivot of the incarnation, the doctrine closest to pastoral work. *Caro salutis est cardo,* wrote Tertullian. "The flesh is the pivot-point of salvation."

XV

Poems

The Greeting

Hail, O favored one,
the Lord is with you!
Luke 1:28

My mail carrier, driving his stubby white
Truck, trimmed in blue and red, wingless
But wheeled, commissioned by the civil service
Daily delivers the Gospel every Advent.

This Gabriel, uniformed in gabardine,
Unsmiling descendant of his dazzling original,
Under the burden of greetings is stoical
But prompt: annunciations at ten each morning.

One or two or three a day at first;
By the second week momentum's up,
My mail box is stuffed, each card stamped

With the glory at a cost of only twenty-five cents,
(Bringing the news that God is here with us)
First class, personally hand addressed.

The Tree

There shall come forth a shoot from the stump of Jesse,
and a branch shall grow out of his roots.
Isaiah 11:1

Jesse's roots, composted with carcasses
Of dove and lamb, parchments of ox and goat,
Centuries of dried up prayers and bloody
Sacrifice, now bear me gospel fruit.

   David's branch, fed on kosher soil,
   Blossoms a messianic flower, and then
   Ripens into a kingdom crop, conserving
   The fragrance and warmth of spring for winter use.

Holy Spirit, shake our family tree;
Release your ripened fruit to our outstretched arms.

   I'd like to see my children sink their teeth
   Into promised land pomegranates

And Canaan grapes, bushel gifts of God,
While I skip a grace rope to a Christ tune.

The Star

I see him, but not now; I behold him, but not nigh:
a star shall come forth out of Jacob.
Numbers 24:17

No star is visible except at night,
Until the sun goes down, no accurate north.
Day's brightness hides what darkness shows to sight,
The hour I go to sleep the bear strides forth.

  I open my eyes to the cursed but requisite dark,
  The black sink that drains my cistern dry,
  And see, not nigh, not now, the heavenly mark
  Exploding in the quasar-messaged sky.

Out of the dark, behind my back, a sun
Launched light-years ago, completes its run;

  The undeciphered skies of myth and story
  Now narrate the cadenced runes of glory.

Lost pilots wait for night to plot their flight,
Just so diurnal pilgrims praise the midnight.

The Candle

The people who walked in darkness have seen a great light:
Those who dwelt in a land of deep darkness, on them
has light shined.
Isaiah 9:2

Uncandled menorahs and oilless lamps abandoned
By foolish virgins too much in a hurry to wait
And tend the light are clues to the failed watch,
The missed arrival, the midnight might-have-been.

   Wick and beeswax make a guttering protest,
   Fragile, defiant flame against demonic
   Terrors that gust, invisible and nameless,
   Out of galactic ungodded emptiness.

Then deep in the blackness fires nursed by wise
Believers surprise with shining all groping derelicts

   Bruised and stumbling in a world benighted.
   The sudden blazing backlights each head with a nimbus.

Shafts of storm-filtered sun search and destroy
The Stygian desolation: I see. I see.

The Time

When the time had fully come, God sent forth his Son,
born of a woman, born under the law, to redeem those
who were under the law, so that we might receive
adoption . . .
Galatians 4:4–5

Half, or more than half, my life is spent
In waiting: waiting for the day to come
When dawn spills laughter's animated sun
Across the rim of God into my tent.

In my other clock sin I put off
Until I'm ready, which I never seem
To be, the seized day, the kingdom dream
Come true. My head has been too long in the trough.

Keeping a steady messianic rhythm,
Ocean tides and woman's blood fathom

The deep that calls to deep, and bring to birth
The seeded years, and grace this wintered earth

Measured by the metronomic moon.
Nothing keeps time better than a womb.

The Dream

. . . an angel of the Lord appeared to him in a dream.
Matthew 1:20

Amiably conversant with virtue and evil,
The righteousness of Joseph and wickedness
Of Herod, I'm ever and always a stranger to grace.
I need this annual angel visitation

— sudden dive by dream to reality —
To know the virgin conceives and God is with us.
The dream powers its way through winter weather
And gives me vision to see the Jesus gift.

Light from the dream lasts a year. Impervious
To equinox and solstice it makes twelve months

Of daylight by which I see the crèche where my
Redeemer lives. Archetypes of praise take shape

Deep in my spirit. As autumn wanes I count
The days 'til I will have the dream again.

The Cradle

And she gave birth to her first-born son and wrapped him
in swaddling clothes, and laid him in a manger.
Luke 2:7

For us who have only known approximate fathers
And mothers manqué, this child is a surprise:
A sudden coming true of all we hoped
Might happen. Hoarded hopes fed by prophecies,

   Old sermons and song fragments, now cry
   Coo and gurgle in the cradle, a babbling
   Proto-language which as soon as it gets
   A tongue (and we, of course, grow open ears)

Will say the big nouns: joy, glory, peace;
And live the best verbs: love, forgive, save.
Along with the swaddling clothes the words are washed

   Of every soiling sentiment, scrubbed clean of
   All failed promises, then hung in the world's
   Backyard dazzling white, billowing gospel.

The Pain

. . . and a sword will pierce through your own soul
also, that thoughts out of many hearts may be revealed.
Luke 2:35

The bawling of babies, always in a way
Inappropriate — why should the loved and innocent
Greet existence with wails? — is proof that not all
Is well. Dreams and deliveries never quite mesh.

    Deep hungers go unsatisfied, deep hurts
    Unhealed. The natural and gay are torn
    By ugly grimace and curse. A wound appears
    In the place of ecstasy. Birth is bloody.

All pain's a prelude: to symphony, to sweetness.
"The pearl began as a pain in the oyster's stomach."

    Dogwood, recycled from cradle to cross, enters
    The market again as a yoke for easing burdens.

Each sword-opened side is the matrix for God
To come to me again through travail for joy.

The War

And the dragon stood before the woman who was
about to bear a child, that he might devour her
child. . . . Now war arose in heaven.
Revelation 12:4, 7

This birth's a signal for war. Lovers fight,
Friends fall out. Merry toasts from flagons
Of punch are swallowed in the maw of dragons.
Will mother and baby survive this devil night?

I've done my share of fighting in the traffic:
Kitchen quarrels, playground fisticuffs;
Every cherub choir has its share of toughs,
And then one day I learned the fight was cosmic.

Truce: I lay down arms; my arms fill up
With gifts: wild and tame, real and stuffed

Lions. Lambs play, oxen low,
The infant fathers festive force. One crow

Croaks defiance into the shalom whiteness,
Empty, satanic bluster against the brightness.

The Carol

*Glory to God in the highest, and on earth peace among
men with whom he is pleased.*
Luke 2:14

Untuned, I'm flat on my feet, sharp with my tongue,
A walking talking dischord, out of sorts,
My heart murmurs are entered in lab reports.
The noise between my ears cannot be sung.

  Ill-pleased, I join a line of hard-to-please people
  Who want to exchange their lumpy bourgeois souls
  For a keen Greek mind with a strong Roman nose,
  Then find ourselves, surprised, at the edge of a stable.

Caroling angels and a well-pleased God
Join a choir of cow and sheep and dog

  At this barnyard border between wish and gift.
  I glimpse the just-formed flesh, now mine. They lift

Praise voices and sing twelve tones
Of pleasure into my muscles, into my bones.

The Feast

He who is mighty has done great things for me. . . .
He has filled the hungry with good things.
Luke 1:49, 53

The milkful breasts brim blessings and quiet
The child into stillness, past pain: El Shaddai
Has done great things for me. Earth nurses
Heaven on the slopes of the Grand Tetons.

  Grown-up, he gives breakfasts, breaks bread,
  Itinerant host at a million feasts.
  His milkfed bones are buried unbroken
  In the Arimethean's tomb.

The world has worked up an appetite:
And comes on the run to the table he set:
Strong meat, full-bodied wine.

  Wassailing with my friends in the winter
  Mountains, I'm back for seconds as often
  As every week: drink long! drink up!

The Dance

When the voice of your greeting came to my ears,
the babe in my womb leaped for joy.
Luke 1:44

Another's heart lays downs the beat that puts
Me in motion, in perichoresis, steps
Learned in the womb before the world's foundation.
It never misses a beat: praise pulses.

Leaping toward the light, I'm dancing in
The dark, touching now the belly of blessing,
Now the aching side, ready for birth,
For naming and living love's mystery out in the open.

The nearly dead and the barely alive pick up
The chthonic rhythms in their unused muscles

And gaily cartwheel three hallelujahs.
But not all: "Those who are deaf always despise

Those who dance." That doesn't stop the dance:
All waiting light leap at the voice of greeting.

The Gift

*For to us a child is born, to us a son is given . . . and his
name will be called "Wonderful Counselor, Mighty God,
Everlasting Father, Prince of Peace."*
Isaiah 9:6

Half-sick with excitement and under garish lights
I do it again, year after year after year.
I can't wait to plunder the boxes, then show
And tell my friends: Look what I got!

    I rip the tissues from every gift but find
    That all the labels have lied. Stones.
    And my heart a stone. "Dead in trespasses
    And sin." The lights go out. Later my eyes,

Accustomed to the dark, see wrapped
In Christ-foil and ribboned in Spirit-colors

    The multi-named messiah, love labels
    On a faith shape, every name a promise

And every promise a present, made and named
All in the same breath. I accept.

The Offering

May the kings of Tarshish and of isles render him tribute,
  may the kings of Sheba and Seba bring gifts!
Long may he live,
  may gold of Sheba be given to him!
Psalm 72:10, 15

Brought up in a world where there's no free lunch
And trained to use presents for barter, I'm spending
The rest of my life receiving this gift with no
Strings attached, but not doing too well.

  Three bathrobed wise men with six or seven
  Inches of jeans and sneakers showing, kneel,
  Offering gifts that symbolize the gifts
  That none of us is ready yet to give.

A few of us stay behind, blow out the candles,
Sweep up the straw and put the creche in storage.

  We open the door into the world's night
  And find we've played ourselves into a better

Performance. We leave with our left-over change changed
At the offertory into kingdom gold.